T H E   B O O K   O F

LIGHT ITALIAN
Dishes

THE BOOK OF

LIGHT ITALIAN
Dishes

MAXINE CLARK

Photographed by
SIMON BUTCHER

HPBooks®

ANOTHER BEST SELLING VOLUME FROM HP BOOKS

HPBooks
Published by The Berkley Publishing Group
200 Madison Avenue
New York, NY 10016

9 8 7 6 5 4 3 2 1

ISBN 1-55788-268-1

By arrangement with Salamander Books Ltd.

Home Economist: Nicola Fowler
Printed in Spain

CONTENTS

INTRODUCTION

Italian cooking brings all the flavors and sunshine of the Mediterranean into your kitchen, and with *The Book of Light Italian Dishes* you can bring all the additional benefits of the Mediterranean diet to your lifestyle. Using olive oil to replace animal fat, and incorporating small amounts of meat and pasta with maximum amounts of fish and vegetables, Italian food can be lightened to suit our hectic modern way of life.

A feast of over 80 recipes, from healthy hearty soups, easy starters, pastas, pizzas and risottos, delicious fish, light poultry and meat dishes, a variety of vegetable accompaniments, to luscious low-fat desserts. Each recipe is illustrated in full color, with clear step-by-step instructions, to make light Italian cooking as quick and easy as possible.

——LIGHT ITALIAN COOKING——

Italian food can be lightened to suit our modern low-fat, high fiber diet without losing the taste and depth of flavor. The use of good quality fresh ingredients is essential for the best flavor and texture. Use ingredients seasonally, when they are freshest and the flavor is most intense.

BREADS, PULSES AND BEANS
Each region of Italy has its own speciality bread from the saltless, and rather tasteless, Tuscan bread to the "ciabatta" or slipper bread made with olive oil, and focaccia in all its shapes and sizes.

Bread is an essential part of any meal in Italy, being both nutritious and filling, and providing essential roughage. It is often toasted over charcoal, rubbed with garlic and drizzled with a little olive oil and served as a starter – the original "bruschetta." Used in crumb form, bread can coat foods, eke out fillings, and protect the surface of food from drying out.

Borlotti, cannellini, black-eyed, kidney and haricot beans are staples throughout Italy (especially in Tuscany), and are used in both hearty soups and simple salads. They are a good source of protein and contain little or no fat.

FISH AND SEAFOOD
All manner of fish and seafood is eaten in Italy, the variety is enormous. Squid, cuttlefish, tuna, swordfish, red mullet, grey mullet, sea bass, sardines, clams, mussels and endless varieties of shrimp are popular.

Although you should eat less of the oily fish like sardines, to cut down on calories, there are benefits in fish oil such as their effect on the breakdown of cholesterol.

Anchovies, whether salted or in oil, are used to give a piquant savouriness to some Italian dishes. Salted anchovies are the whole fish (without head) preserved in salt, and need to be rinsed and the backbone removed before using. Anchovies preserved in oil should be rinsed well before using. They are very strong in flavor, so use sparingly.

Fish is often cooked on a barbecue, but it is also steamed, poached, and quickly fried – a nonstick frying pan is good for frying with little or no added fat.

GAME AND MEAT
Game is universally popular – rabbit, hare, wild boar and partridge to name but a few. It is low in fat, free-range, and has lots of taste. Most chicken dishes can be made with all types of game bird, and the flavor will be much stronger. Tuscans often eat meat and balance it with beans and vegetables, whereas Sicilians prefer fish. Beef and veal should be eaten in small quantities, and turkey can

often be substituted for veal. Pork is bred to be lean nowadays and is not so fat ridden as it once was – it is made into all sorts of products, which used judiciously can add a lot of flavor to many different dishes.

HAM AND BACON

Prosciutto is the generic term for ham. Prosciutto crudo is raw cured ham, and Parma ham is a particularly high quality prosciutto crudo. Pancetta is unsmoked Italian bacon, rolled up and sliced to order. It is a dry cure and smoked bacon does not give the same flavor. Cut off as much fat as possible before using these products. Drain off any fat released during cooking if really concerned about cholesterol.

ITALIAN SAUSAGES

These are freshly made with coarsely ground pork, a little fat and highly seasoned with salt and pepper. They are often flavored with fennel, chile, basil and pine nuts.

GARLIC

The larger the cloves of garlic, the sweeter it will be. Small hard heads of garlic tend to be bitter and strong. The softer and fresher the garlic, the more subtle the flavor. Avoid mean garlic heads in little boxes! Garlic is used in many ways to give a vast range of flavors.

HERBS

Parsley, basil, sage, rosemary, thyme, bay, mint and oregano are widely used

to enhance flavor without adding calories. Fresh herbs are always better than dried. Capers are the flower bud of the caper plant which grows wild all over Italy. The buds are either salted or preserved in vinegar. The larger seed pods are used too – they add a piquancy to salads and sauces.

SALADS AND VEGETABLES

All kinds of salad greens, both wild and cultivated, are eaten, and Italian markets spill over with tempting greenery in the summer. Salads are a very important part of the meal, no matter how small the portion – often it is just a few salad greens to cleanse the palate. They are very often quite bitter leaves like arugula, radicchio, romaine and chicory.

Popular vegetables in Italy are beans, squashes, eggplant, fennel, zucchini and their flowers, which can be stuffed, potatoes, and bell peppers.

TOMATOES

Although relative newcomers to Italian cuisine, tomatoes have become an essential ingredient. Fresh tomatoes should be slightly soft, bright red and sweet. Canned and bottled tomatoes are essential in the winter when fresh are not available. Sun-dried tomatoes are used sparingly in Italian cooking. Tomato paste adds richness and Sicilian "strattu," a clay-like sun-dried concentrate of tomatoes, is a real find – a little goes a long way.

WILD MUSHROOMS

The most famous and much-prized mushroom is the "porcini" or "cep" or "Penny Bun". It is gathered in the wild and much coveted. Both fresh and dried are expensive, but one or two dried mushrooms (after soaking) add great flavor to risottos and sauces, and are very low in fat.

OLIVES

Olives are a much prized crop, picked late in the year when green, or left to ripen on the tree until black or purple. Olive oil is synonymous with Italian cuisine, and the choice is limitless. Choose a cold-pressed fruity, extra virgin olive oil with a low acidity (less than 1%) for dressing salads, and a lighter less expensive oil for cooking and baking. A dark green olive oil does not necessarily guarantee quality – taste it and see. Olive pastes are rich and salty and can be used sparingly as toppings, bread and pasta flavorings or even whisked into a dressing. Olive oil has a high fat content, but is monosaturated fat which is healthier than animal fats. Use it in moderation to enhance the flavor of foods. It is good with lemon juice and vinegar.

BALSAMIC VINEGAR

This rich sweet vinegar is made from fermented Trebbiano grapes, aged in oak casks for at least 4 years (and some vinegars for much longer). It is a boon to lighter cooking as it lends a subtle richness to a dish without the fat! There is no real substitute, but sherry vinegar is the nearest thing. Balsamic vinegar is especially good sprinkled over strawberries.

PASTA

Egg pasta is traditionally made with Italian "00" flour (Farina Tipo 00) – the finest, whitest grade of Italian "grano tenero" or soft grain flour, eggs, olive oil and salt. The "00" flour is sometimes mixed with "semolino di grano duro" or semolina flour. This is made from the heart of the wheat, has a high gluten content and is the flour used for making commercial dried pasta. Most commercially dried pasta is made from "grano duro" or hard-wheat or semolina flour and water. This contains much less cholesterol than "pasta al'uovo" made with eggs.

Semolina flour gives dried pasta a firmer texture. It is also good for "flouring" fresh pasta as it is coarser than flour, aerates it prior to cooking,

and does not stick to the pasta during cooking.

Pasta is very versatile and is great value for money as far as satisfying hunger is concerned. In Italy, the pasta is tossed in the sauce to just coat, along with a little of the cooking water which helps to emulsify the sauce. It is never swamped in sauce, just flavored with it.

Pasta is essentially a food of the poor, cheap while satisfying hunger and providing a good source of slow and constantly released energy. It contains more carbohydrate and protein than potatoes.

Whole-wheat pasta is not eaten much in Italy, but it is extremely nutritious and slightly lower in calories than ordinary dried pasta. Buy good quality pasta – dried pasta is often better quality than fresh. Eaten in moderation, it can liven up your diet.

FLOUR

Italian breads such as focaccia are made with all-purpose flour; bread flour makes the dough too elastic and gives the wrong texture.

POLENTA FLOUR (Farina Giallo)

This coarsely ground maize is used for making soft polenta like mashed potato and the firmer sliced and grilled polenta to serve with grilled and roasted meats. It takes about 40 minutes to cook, but "quick cook" or "instant" polenta, which is ready in 5-10 minutes, is a good substitute.

RICE

Arborio rice for risotto is the most widely available exported Italian rice. It is a short grain rice with good absorption and is essential for making creamy risottos. It is the fat and cheese in risottos that make them high in calories, not the rice itself, which is very nutritious.

FRUIT AND NUTS

Italians love fruit, whether served raw, cooked or in a salad. Best of all, fruit is eaten with great gusto in sorbets and ice creams. Sorbets are good for a healthy diet as they contain little fat and, served in small quantities, are very refreshing. They were one of the many Arab contributions to Italian cuisine.

Lemons, oranges, watermelon, melon, apricots, peaches, pears, apples, nectarines, plums, persimmons, wild strawberries, raspberries, grapes, fresh walnuts, hazelnuts, chestnuts, and almonds are some of the wide choice available to Italians. Preserved fruits such as candied citrus peel are widely used in baking and desserts.

Almonds, walnuts and hazelnuts are extensively used in Italian desserts and candies, but have been kept to a minimum in the recipes in this book to reduce calories. Pine nuts, the seeds of pine cones, are expensive as their extraction is labor-intensive. They are generally not toasted, but are quite high in calories, so use them sparingly.

DAIRY PRODUCTS

Cheeses and dairy products are used widely in Northern Italian cooking, quite lavishly. Try to use low or reduced fat versions where possible. Use low-fat or skimmed milk and light cream instead of heavy cream. Low-fat yogurts or fromage frais are good substitutes for creamy, melting cheeses.

Fresh mozzarella is a favorite ingredient for salads and pizzas. The best is made from water buffalo milk. It melts to a delicious stringiness when heated. Parmigiano (Parmesan) is a hard "grana" cheese. It is salty and crumbly, and a pale straw color. Parmigiano Reggiano is the best, but Grana Padano is good in cooking. Shaving fine curls of Parmesan onto salads is a current fashion. Although Parmesan is high in fat, a little goes a long way.

Mascarpone is a fresh thick cheese made from cream, and mainly used in desserts – ricotta cheese mixed with low-fat yogurt could be substituted. Ricotta is a cheese made from whey and should be snowy white and sweet. Reduced-fat ricotta is used in the recipes in this book.

EGGS

Free-range farm eggs in Italy have amazingly bright yellow yolks – a result of feeding corn – and make wonderful yellow omelettes and pasta Try to limit your intake of eggs as the yolks have a high cholesterol and fat content.

SPICES AND FLOWER WATERS

The Romans used fennel and poppyseeds to flavor breads, but it was in the Renaissance, when the Venetians were the center of the spice trade with the East, that spices became widely used. Saffron, cinnamon, nutmeg, vanilla, aniseed, cloves, black and white pepper, mace and ginger were used to mask the taste of rotting food, and as preservatives. Orange flower water and rosewater were brought to Sicily by the Arabs and feature heavily in candies and desserts.

WINE

Enjoying Italian food without wine would be almost sacrilegious, and there is no reason why some wine should not be part of your healthy, low-fat diet. Many sauces and desserts contain wine in modest amounts.

──TUSCAN BEAN SOUP──

8 oz. dried white beans (haricot, cannellini),
  soaked overnight
2 tablespoons chopped fresh sage or rosemary
5 tablespoons olive oil
2 cloves garlic, finely chopped
Salt and freshly ground pepper
2 cloves garlic, finely sliced
1 fresh red chile, cored, seeded and chopped
chopped fresh parsley, to garnish

Preheat oven to 325F (165C). Drain beans and place in a flameproof casserole. Cover with water to a depth of 2 inches above the beans.

Bring to a boil, cover tightly and bake in the oven for about 1 hour or until tender. Remove from the oven and allow to cool slightly in the cooking liquid. Place half the beans and liquid in a food processor or blender and process until smooth. Stir into the beans in the casserole with the sage or rosemary. Add extra water if too thick. Heat 2 tablespoons olive oil in a frying pan and fry the chopped garlic until soft and golden. Stir it into the soup, reheat until boiling, then simmer gently 10 minutes.

Taste the soup and season well with salt and pepper. Heat remaining olive oil in the frying pan and fry the sliced garlic and the chile until golden. Pour soup into soup plates or bowls, spoon garlic and chile over the top and sprinkle with chopped parsley. Serve at once.

Makes 6 servings.

Total Cals: 1185   Total fat: 60 g
Cals per portion: 198   Fat per portion: 10 g

——— PASTA & BEAN SOUP ———

6 oz. (1 cup) dried haricot beans, soaked
  overnight
2 cloves garlic, crushed
7½ cups chicken stock or water
¾ cup medium pasta shells
4 tomatoes, peeled, seeded and chopped
4 tablespoons chopped fresh parsley
Salt and freshly ground pepper

Drain beans and place in a saucepan with
garlic and chicken stock or water. Simmer,
half-covered, 2 to 2½ hours or until tender.

Allow to cool slightly, then transfer beans
and cooking liquid to a food processor or
blender and puree. Return puree to the pan,
add pasta and tomatoes and simmer gently
15 minutes until tender. (Add a little extra
chicken stock or water if the soup is too
thick.)

Stir in chopped parsley and season well with
salt and pepper. Serve at once.

Makes 6 servings.

Total Cals: 1045   Total fat: 7.3 g
Cals per portion: 174   Fat per portion: 1.2 g

MINESTRONE

2 tablespoons olive oil
2 oz. lightly smoked streaky bacon, diced
2 large onions, peeled and sliced
2 garlic cloves, skinned and crushed
2 medium carrots, peeled and diced
3 stalks celery, trimmed and sliced
1¼ cup dried haricot beans, soaked
1 (14½-oz.) can chopped tomatoes
10 cups beef stock
4 oz. frozen green peas
12 oz. potatoes, peeled and diced
6 oz. small pasta shapes
8 oz. green cabbage, thinly sliced
6 oz. green beans, trimmed and sliced
3 tablespoons each chopped fresh parsley and basil
Salt and freshly ground pepper

Heat oil in a large saucepan and add bacon, onions, and garlic. Cover and cook gently for 5 minutes, stirring occasionally until soft but not colored. Add carrots and celery and cook 2 to 3 minutes until softening. Drain beans and add to the pan with tomatoes and stock. Cover and simmer 1 to 1½ hours, until beans are nearly tender.

Add peas and potatoes and cook for a further 15 minutes, then add the pasta, cabbage, beans and chopped parsley and cook for a further 15 minutes. Stir in the basil, adjust seasoning and serve.

Makes 8 servings.

Total Cals: 2488	Total fat: 57.4 g
Cals per portion: 311	Fat per portion: 7.2 g

Note: Serve with freshly grated Parmesan cheese, if desired.

ZUCCHINI SOUP

2 tablespoons olive or sunflower oil
2 medium sweet onions, finely chopped
6¼ cups chicken stock
2 lbs. zucchini, trimmed and grated
Fresh lemon juice, to taste
Salt and freshly ground pepper
2 tablespoons chopped fresh chervil or tarragon
⅔ cup low-fat yogurt, to serve

Heat oil in a large saucepan and add onions. Cover and cook gently about 20 minutes until they are very soft but not colored, stirring occasionally.

Pour in stock and bring to a boil. Stir in zucchini and bring to a boil again, then turn down the heat and simmer 15 minutes. Season to taste with lemon juice, salt and pepper.

Stir in chopped chervil or tarragon, add a swirl of yogurt and serve at once.

Makes 6 servings.

Total Cals: 497   Total fat: 26.9 g
Cals per portion: 83   Fat per portion: 4.5 g

──── ROASTED PEPPER SOUP ────

6 yellow bell peppers
4 medium leeks, white and pale green parts only,
  thinly sliced
2 tablespoons olive oil
3 cups chicken stock
Salt and freshly ground pepper
Toasted country bread, to serve

Preheat oven to 475F (245C). Place bell peppers in a large roasting pan and roast in the oven 20 to 30 minutes until they begin to char, turning once. Remove from oven and place in a plastic bag, closing tightly. Let stand 10 minutes.

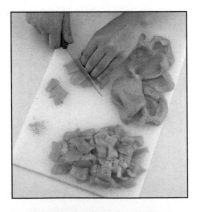

Meanwhile, place sliced leeks in a bowl of cold water to soak 5 minutes. Remove bell peppers from the bag and scrape off skins. Pull out the cores and the seeds should come with them. Halve the bell peppers, scrape out any remaining seeds and roughly chop the flesh. Drain the leeks.

Heat oil, add leeks and cook them gently for 10 minutes until soft but not colored. Add bell peppers, stock and season with salt and pepper. Bring to a boil then turn down the heat and simmer 20 minutes. Puree in a blender, then pass through a sieve into the rinsed-out pan. Reheat, taste and season. Serve with toasted country bread.

Makes 4 servings

Total Cals: 573   Total fat: 26.1 g
Cals per portion: 143   Fat per portion: 6.5 g

PUMPKIN SOUP

1 (1½-lb.) fresh pumpkin
6 cloves garlic, unpeeled
4 tablespoons olive oil
2 medium leeks, finely sliced and washed
1 stalk celery, chopped
¼ cup long grain white rice
6¼ cups vegetable or chicken stock or water
Salt and freshly ground pepper
4 tablespoons chopped fresh parsley
Parsley sprigs, to garnish

Preheat oven to 400F (205C). Scrape out seeds from pumpkin, cut off the skin and cut flesh into large cubes.

Place pumpkin in a roasting pan with garlic cloves and toss with 2 tablespoons olive oil. Do not crowd pan – use 2 pans if necessary. Roast in oven 30 minutes until tender and beginning to brown. Meanwhile, heat remaining olive oil in a large saucepan, add leeks and celery and cook over low heat 10 minutes until just beginning to brown and soften. Stir in the rice, stock or water, bring to a boil, cover and simmer about 15 to 20 minutes until rice is tender.

Remove pumpkin from oven, cool slightly, then press garlic cloves out of skins. Add the garlic and pumpkin to rice, bring to a boil and simmer 10 minutes. Puree in a blender and return to pan. Season with plenty of black pepper. Add extra stock or water if the soup is too thick. Reheat and stir in chopped parsley. Serve garnished with parsley sprigs.

Makes 6 servings.

Total Cals: 805   Total fat: 49 g
Cals per portion: 134   Fat per portion: 8.3 g

CHICKPEA SOUP

14 oz. (2 cups) dried chickpeas, soaked
  overnight
1 tablespoon chopped fresh rosemary
2 fresh bay leaves
2 cloves garlic, peeled and halved
3 oz. pancetta or smoked lean bacon, chopped
2 medium onions, finely chopped
1 carrot, chopped
1 stalk celery, chopped
Salt and freshly ground black pepper
Rosemary sprigs, to garnish

Drain chickpeas, place in a saucepan with
the rosemary, bay and garlic.

Cover with fresh water and bring to a boil.
Cover pan and simmer chickpeas about 40
minutes until tender. Meanwhile, heat a
nonstick frying pan, add pancetta or bacon
and fry over medium heat until fat begins to
run. Add chopped vegetables and cook for 5
to 10 minutes until they are beginning to
soften and brown.

Drain chickpeas, reserve cooking liquid and
return chickpeas to the pan. Stir in pancetta
and vegetables and enough of reserved cooking liquid to cover. Bring to a boil, half-
cover, reduce heat and simmer chickpeas 30
minutes until starting to fall apart and
thicken the soup, stirring occasionally. Taste
and season. Serve garnished with rosemary.

Makes 6 servings.

Total Cals: 698   Total fat: 18.1 g
Cals per portion: 116   Fat per portion: 3 g

PAPPA AL POMODORO

4 tablespoons olive oil
1 onion, finely chopped
3 cloves garlic, finely chopped
2¾ lbs. very ripe tomatoes, chopped
6¾ cups vegetable, chicken or meat stock
14 oz. stale breadcrumbs
2 oz. fresh basil leaves, shredded
Salt and freshly ground black pepper

Heat half the oil in a medium saucepan, add onion and garlic and cook over low heat 5 minutes until softened. Stir in tomatoes, bring to a boil and simmer 10 minutes.

Transfer the mixture to a food processor or blender and puree. Pass the puree through a sieve into a large saucepan, then whisk in the stock.

Slowly bring to boil and stir in breadcrumbs and half the basil. Season to taste with salt and pepper. Reduce heat, cover and simmer about 45 minutes or until thick and creamy, stirring occasionally. Stir in remaining oil and basil, check seasoning and serve at once.

Makes 8 servings.

Total Cals: 2141   Total fat: 56 g
Cals per portion: 268   Fat per portion: 7 g

MUSSEL SOUP

2 tablespoons olive oil
3 cloves garlic, 2 chopped and 1 whole
8 oz. ripe tomatoes, chopped
Pinch of hot chile powder
6 slices country bread
3 cups fish or vegetable stock
3 lbs. mussels, scrubbed and de-bearded
3 tablespoons chopped fresh parsley

Heat the oil in a large Dutch oven, add chopped garlic and cook until golden. Stir in the tomatoes and chile powder. Cover and simmer 25 minutes until the oil separates.

Cut whole garlic clove in half. Toast bread on both sides and rub each side with a cut side of the garlic clove.

Add stock to the pan and bring to a boil. Add mussels, cover and cook 3 to 5 minutes until all the mussels are open, occasionally shaking the pan. Scatter parsley over the top and serve with the garlic bread.

Makes 6 servings.

Total Cals: 1026   Total fat: 38.9 g
Cals per portion: 171   Fat per portion: 6.3 g

Variation: Substitute clams for the mussels.

FENNEL SOUP

¼ cup olive oil
1 medium onion, chopped
8 oz. fennel, peeled, cored and thinly sliced,
  reserving any green fronds for garnish
1 potato, diced
3 cups chicken stock
Salt and freshly ground pepper
Fresh lemon juice, to taste

Heat oil in a large saucepan and add onion.
Cook 5 minutes until onion is beginning to
soften. Add fennel and potato and cook 5
minutes until fennel begins to soften.

Pour in chicken stock and bring to a boil.
Turn down heat, cover and simmer about 45
minutes. Puree in a blender and pass it
through a sieve into the rinsed-out pan.

Reheat soup, taste and season well with salt,
pepper and lemon juice. Garnish with the
reserved fennel fronds and serve at once.

Makes 6 servings.

Total Cals: 556   Total fat: 39.7 g
Cals per portion: 93   Fat per portion: 6.6 g

—PEPPERS WITH ARTICHOKES—

6 red, orange or yellow bell peppers
12 frozen artichoke hearts, thawed or 12 artichokes
  canned in brine, drained
24 anchovy fillets, drained
6 tablespoons extra-virgin olive oil
Salt and freshly ground pepper
4 cloves garlic, sliced
2 tablespoons chopped fresh oregano

Preheat broiler. Arrange the whole peppers in a broiler pan and roast under broiler until the skin begins to char. Turn the peppers until they are evenly charred. Slip off the skins while still warm.

Cut peppers in half lengthways and scrape out the seeds. Place the peppers cut side up in a shallow serving dish. Cut the artichoke hearts in half and place two halves in each pepper. Arrange 2 anchovy fillets over each pepper half. Spoon a little olive oil over each artichoke.

Season with salt and pepper, then scatter the sliced garlic and oregano over the top. Cover and refrigerate overnight for the flavors to meld. Allow to come to room temperature before serving with crusty Italian bread.

Makes 6 servings.

Total Cals: 1762   Total fat: 149 g
Cals per portion: 294   Fat per portion: 24.9 g

——— TOMATO BRUSCHETTA ———

9 oz. part-skim mozzarella, cut into small cubes
20 cherry tomatoes, quartered
3 tablespoons olive oil
1 teaspoon balsamic or sherry vinegar
Salt and freshly ground pepper
6 thick slices country bread
2 garlic cloves, skinned
4 oz. arugula or watercress
Generous handful of fresh basil leaves, to garnish

Place mozzarella in a bowl with tomatoes. Whisk together olive oil and vinegar, season with salt and pepper and pour it over the cheese and tomatoes. Mix well.

Toast the bread on both sides and keep it warm. Cut the garlic cloves in half and rub each slice of toasted bread with a cut side of garlic clove.

Place a slice of toast on each of 6 plates and surround each slice with arugula or watercress. Pile the mozzarella and tomato mixture on top of the toast, garnish with fresh basil leaves and serve.

Makes 6 servings.

Total Cals: 1386   Total fat: 76.6 g
Cals per portion: 231   Fat per portion: 12.7 g

—GRILLED PROSCIUTTO & FIGS—

8 fresh ripe figs
3 tablespoons olive oil
12 thin slices of prosciutto or Parma ham
3 tablespoons freshly grated Parmesan cheese
Crushed black pepper, to serve

Take each fig and stand it upright. Using a sharp knife, make 2 cuts across and downwards in each fig not quite quartering it, but keeping it intact. Ease the figs open and brush with olive oil.

Place the figs cut side down on a hot grill or ridged griddle and cook for 5 to 10 minutes until hot and golden brown, turning once. Alternatively, place under a very hot broiler and broil until brown and hot through. While the figs are cooking, place half the prosciutto slices on the grill or griddle and grill 2 to 3 minutes until starting to crisp. Remove and keep warm while cooking the remaining slices.

Arrange 3 pieces of the ham and 2 figs per person on warm plates. Sprinkle with grated Parmesan and season with plenty of crushed black pepper. Serve at once.

Makes 4 servings.

Total Cals: 847   Total fat: 53.7 g
Cals per portion: 212   Fat per portion: 13 g

──CHICKEN LIVER CROSTINI──

8 oz. fresh chicken livers
2 tablespoons olive oil
2 medium leeks, white parts only, washed and finely
  chopped
1 stalk celery, finely chopped
1 tablespoon balsamic or sherry vinegar
2 tablespoons capers in brine, drained
1/3 cup chicken stock
1 tablespoon chopped fresh thyme
Salt and freshly ground pepper
12 slices French bread, toasted on both sides
Thyme sprigs, to garnish

Rinse livers, removing gristle or discolored bits. Dry on paper towels.

Heat olive oil in a nonstick frying pan, add leeks and celery and cook 5 minutes until soft but not colored. Add chicken livers and fry them with the vegetables about 5 minutes. Sprinkle with the vinegar and allow it to evaporate over the heat.

Stir in the capers, chicken stock and thyme and bring to a boil. Season well with salt and pepper. Reduce heat and simmer 10 to 15 minutes until thickened and creamy, stirring all the time. Spread the mixture on the warm toasted bread and serve at once, garnished with thyme sprigs.

Makes 6 servings.

Total Cals: 1851   Total fat: 50 g
Cals per portion: 308   Fat per portion: 8.4 g

—PEPPER & ANCHOVY SALAD—

3 each large red and yellow bell peppers
⅓ cup olive oil or olive oil and sunflower oil mixed
1 tablespoon wine or balsamic vinegar
Salt and freshly ground pepper
1 (2-oz.) can anchovies, drained, rinsed and
  chopped
4 oz. ripe olives, stoned
3 to 4 tablespoons chopped fresh parsley
2 hard-boiled eggs

Preheat oven to 475F (245C). Place peppers in a large roasting pan and roast in oven 20 to 30 minutes until they begin to char, turning once.

Remove peppers from the oven and place in a plastic bag, closing tightly. Let stand 10 minutes, then remove them from the bag and scrape off the skins. Pull out the cores and the seeds should come with them. Halve peppers, scrape out any remaining seeds then cut the flesh into wide strips. Put oil, vinegar, salt, pepper, anchovies, olives and parsley into a large bowl and mix well. Add peppers and toss to coat thoroughly.

Halve eggs and remove yolks. Roughly chop whites and scatter them over the peppers. Sieve the yolks and sprinkle them over the whites. Chill before serving.

Makes 6 to 8 servings.

Total Cals: 1138   Total fat: 90.6 g
Cals per portion: 190   Fat per portion: 15 g

──GARLIC & LEMON SHRIMP──

8 oz. small to medium raw shrimp
Salt and freshly ground pepper
4 tablespoons olive oil
2 tablespoons sunflower oil
3 large cloves garlic, coarsely chopped
1 dried red chile pepper, stem and seeds removed,
  chopped
Fresh lemon juice
2 tablespoons chopped fresh parsley
Crusty bread, to serve

Shell shrimp and pat dry on paper towels.
Lay shrimp in a dish and sprinkle lightly
with salt.

Heat the oil in a nonstick frying pan, add
garlic and chile and fry 1 to 2 minutes until
garlic is golden. Immediately add shrimp and
cook over high heat for 2 minutes until the
shrimp are just pink. Add lemon juice to
taste and season with pepper.

Stir in chopped fresh parsley, then serve the
shrimp in ramekins, hot or cold with plenty
of crusty bread.

Makes 4 servings.

Total Cals: 775
Cal per portion: 194

Total fat: 67 g
Fat per portion: 16.9 g

PANZANELLA

7 oz. country bread, crusts removed and cubed
6 tomatoes, coarsely chopped
1 red onion, chopped
½ cucumber, seeds removed and cubed
2 stalks celery, sliced
4 tablespoons olive oil
1 tablespoon wine vinegar
Salt and freshly ground pepper
2 oz. fresh basil, torn

Place bread cubes in a bowl and sprinkle lightly with just enough water to moisten them. Let stand 5 minutes.

Add all the vegetables to the bread and toss until well mixed. Sprinkle with the oil and vinegar and season with salt and pepper. Toss again.

Add basil and toss the salad. Transfer to a serving bowl and let stand in a cool place 20 minutes; do not leave it longer or the salad will be mushy. Serve at room temperature.

Makes 6 servings.

Total Cals: 1039   Total fat: 50.4 g
Cals per portion: 173   Fat per portion: 8.4 g

——TUNA & CAPER PÂTÉ——

1 (7-oz.) can tuna in water, drained
4 tablespoons low-fat ricotta or curd cheese
Grated peel of 1 lemon
2 tablespoons freshly squeezed lemon juice
2 tablespoons olive oil
1 tablespoon capers in brine, drained and rinsed
1 clove garlic, finely chopped
1 teaspoon chopped fresh thyme
Salt and freshly ground black pepper
Toasted bread or prepared raw vegetables, to serve
Thyme sprigs, to garnish (optional)

Place the tuna in a bowl and mash with a fork. Beat in the ricotta, lemon peel, lemon juice, olive oil, capers, garlic and thyme until creamy. Taste and season with salt and pepper.

To serve, spread the pâté on slices of toasted bread. Alternatively, serve it as a dip with a selection of raw vegetables. Garnish with thyme sprigs, if desired.

Makes 4 servings.

Total Cals: 462   Total fat: 25.9 g
Cals per portion: 115   Fat per portion: 6.5 g

─────BEAN & BEEF SALAD─────

1 lb. fresh young unshelled broad beans
6 slices Bresaola (Italian dry cured beef fillet)
4 oz. pecorino cheese
2 tablespoons olive oil
1 tablespoon freshly squeezed lemon juice
1 teaspoon chopped fresh oregano
2 tablespoons chopped fresh parsley
Pinch dried red pepper flakes
Salt and freshly ground pepper

Remove broad beans from their shells and blanch in boiling water 20 seconds. Drain, refresh in cold water and pop the beans out of their skins. Place in a bowl.

Cube the pecorino cheese and cut the beef into strips. Add to the beans in the bowl.

Add olive oil, lemon juice, oregano, parsley and pepper flakes. Toss together, taste and season with salt and pepper. Serve immediately.

Makes 6 servings.

Total Cals: 1115	Total fat: 68 g
Cals per portion: 186	Fat per portion: 11.3 g

Variation: Instead of fresh beans, use 6 oz. thawed frozen broad beans. Do not blanch, simply pop them out of their skins.

—TUNA, BEAN & ONION SALAD —

6 oz. dried white haricot or cannellini beans,
  soaked overnight
2 tablespoons olive oil
1 tablespoon sunflower oil
1 teaspoon balsamic vinegar
Salt and freshly ground pepper
1 small red onion, finely sliced
1 leek, white and light green parts finely sliced
1 tablespoon chopped fresh parsley
1 (7-oz.) can tuna in water, drained
1 tablespoon chopped fresh chives

Drain and rinse beans. Place in a saucepan
and cover with cold water.

Bring to a boil, turn down the heat, cover
and simmer 1 to 1½ hours or until beans are
tender but not falling apart. Drain. Whisk
together the oils, vinegar, salt and pepper
and mix into the hot beans.

Stir in the onion, leek, parsley and then the
tuna, being careful not to break up the tuna
too much. Refrigerate until cooled, then
transfer mixture to a serving dish, sprinkle
with the chopped chives and serve.

Makes 4 servings.

Total Cal: 1048   Total fat: 37.8 g
Cals per portion: 262   Fat per portion: 9.4 g

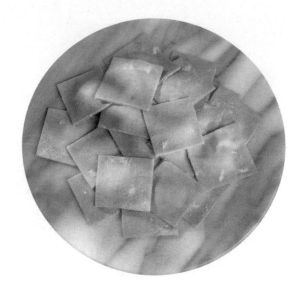

——————BASIC EGG PASTA——————

1¾ cups all-purpose plain white flour
Pinch of salt
2 large eggs, beaten
1 teaspoon olive oil

To make pasta by hand, sift flour and salt onto a clean surface and make a well in the center. Beat eggs and oil together and pour into well. Gradually mix eggs into flour with the fingers of one hand. Knead the pasta about 10 minutes until smooth, wrap and allow to rest at least 30 minutes before rolling out by hand or machine.

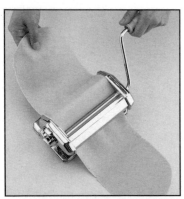

Or, put ingredients in a food processor and process until dough begins to come together. Turn out and knead 10 minutes until smooth. Wrap in plastic wrap and rest 30 minutes, then roll out on a lightly floured surface until thin enough to read newsprint through it. Alternatively, to roll out in a pasta machine, feed dough several times through widest setting first, then pass pasta through machine, reducing settings until reaching right thickness. Generally, second from last setting is best for tagliatelle; the finest for ravioli or pasta to be filled.

Hang the pasta over a broom handle to dry slightly (ravioli should be made at once as it needs to be slightly sticky). Pass the pasta through chosen cutters and transfer to a tray covered with a clean towel sprinkled with a little flour. Toss pasta lightly in the flour and use as soon as possible. Or, drape pasta over broom handle until ready to cook.

Makes 4 servings.

Total Cals: 893   Total fat: 19.1 g
Cals per portion: 223   Fat per portion: 4.8 g

PASTA NAPOLETANA

2 lbs. fresh tomatoes, or 2 (14-oz.) cans plum
  tomatoes with juice, chopped
1 medium onion, finely chopped
1 medium carrot, finely diced
1 stalk celery, diced
⅔ cup dry white wine (optional)
Parsley sprig
Salt and freshly ground pepper
Pinch of sugar
1 tablespoon chopped fresh oregano
12 oz. dried pasta of your choice
Freshly grated Parmesan cheese, to serve (optional)

Put vegetables, wine, parsley, salt, pepper
and sugar in a medium saucepan.

Bring to a boil and simmer, half-covered, 45
minutes until very thick, stirring occasionally. Pass mixture through a sieve or puree in
a blender and sieve to remove the tomato
seeds. Stir in the chopped oregano, then
taste and adjust the seasoning, if necessary.
Reheat gently.

Bring a large pan of salted water to a boil
and cook pasta according to package
instructions until *al dente* (tender but firm to
the bite). Drain well and toss with the hot
sauce. Serve at once, with grated Parmesan
cheese if desired.

Makes 4 servings.

Total Cals: 1529   Total fat: 9.4 g
Cals per portion: 382   Fat per portion: 2.4 g

——SPAGHETTI WITH GARLIC——

5 tablespoons olive oil
Salt and freshly ground pepper
2 cloves garlic, finely chopped
1 red chile, seeded and chopped
14 oz. dried spaghettini or spaghetti
2 tablespoons chopped fresh parsley

Heat oil in a medium saucepan. Add garlic and a pinch of salt and cook very gently until golden, stirring all the time. Do not allow the garlic to become too brown or it will taste bitter. Add chopped chile and cook 1 minute.

Bring a large pan of salted water to a boil and cook pasta according to package instructions until *al dente* (tender but firm to the bite). Drain well.

Toss pasta with the warm, not sizzling, garlic and chile oil and add plenty of black pepper and the parsley. Serve immediately.

Makes 6 servings.

Total Cals: 1862   Total fat: 62 g
Cals per portion: 310   Fat per portion: 10 g

────PASTA CARBONARA────

4 oz. smoked lean bacon or pancetta in a piece
1 clove garlic, finely chopped
10 oz. dried spaghetti or other ribbon pasta
3 eggs, beaten
Salt and freshly ground pepper
3 tablespoons freshly grated Parmesan cheese

Dice bacon and place in a medium saucepan with the garlic. Cook over medium heat until brown. Keep warm.

Bring a large saucepan of salted water to a boil and cook pasta according to package instructions until *al dente* (tender but still firm to the bite). Drain well. Quickly turn the spaghetti into the pan with the bacon.

Stir in eggs, a little salt, lots of pepper and half the cheese. Toss well to mix. The eggs should lightly cook with the heat from the spaghetti. Serve in warm bowls with the remaining cheese.

Makes 4 servings.

Total Cals: 1576   Total fat: 40 g
Cal per portion: 394   Fat per portion: 10 g

PASTA BOLOGNESE

3 oz. pancetta or bacon in a piece, diced
1 medium onion, finely chopped
1 medium carrot, finely diced
1 celery stalk, finely chopped
8 oz. lean ground beef
4 oz. chicken livers, trimmed and chopped
1 medium potato, grated
2 tablespoons tomato paste
½ cup white wine
1 cup beef stock or water
Salt and freshly ground pepper
Freshly grated nutmeg
14 oz. dried spaghetti, fettuccine or tagliatelle
Freshly grated Parmesan cheese, to serve (optional)

Heat a saucepan over medium heat and add pancetta. Cook 2 to 3 minutes until browned. Add onion, carrot and celery and cook until browned. Stir in beef and cook over high heat, breaking it up with a wooden spoon. Stir in the chicken livers and cook them 2 to 3 minutes.

Add potato, tomato paste, mix well and pour in wine and stock. Season with salt, pepper and nutmeg. Bring to a boil, half-cover and simmer 35 minutes until reduced and thickened, stirring occasionally. Meanwhile, cook pasta in boiling salted water until tender. Drain well and toss with sauce. Serve with Parmesan cheese, if desired.

Makes 6 servings.

Total Cals: 2233   Total fat: 37.9 g
Cals per portion: 372   Fat per portion: 6 g

—PUMPKIN RAVIOLI IN BROTH—

1 lb. fresh pumpkin, skin on but seeds
  removed, thickly sliced
2 egg yolks
1½ oz. freshly grated Parmesan cheese
5 fresh sage leaves, chopped
½ teaspoon salt
Pinch of freshly grated nutmeg
2 recipes Basic Egg Pasta (see page 32)
beaten egg for brushing
3¾ cups hot chicken stock
Extra sage leaves, to garnish

Preheat oven to 175F (180C). Boil pumpkin
in salted water 20 minutes until soft. Drain
well and place on a baking sheet.

Bake 10 to 15 minutes to dry out but not
brown. Scoop flesh from the skin, cool, then
mash with egg yolks, cheese, sage, salt and
nutmeg. Spoon into a pastry bag. Halve
dough and wrap one half in plastic wrap.
Roll out dough thinly to a rectangle on a
lightly floured surface. Cover with a clean
damp cloth towel and repeat with the
remaining pasta. Pipe small mounds of filling
in even rows, spacing them at 1½-inch inter-
vals across one piece of the dough. With a
pastry brush, brush the spaces of dough
between the mounds with beaten egg.

Lift remaining pasta over filling. Press down
between pockets of filling. Cut into squares
with a serrated cutter or sharp knife, transfer
to a floured cloth towel and rest 1 hour.
Bring a large saucepan of salted water to a
boil. Toss in ravioli and cook 3 minutes until
puffy, then drain well. Serve with the hot
stock, garnished with sage leaves.

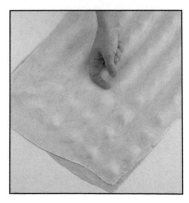

Makes 6 servings.

Total Cals: 2137	Total fat: 63.7 g
Cals per portion: 356	Fat per portion: 10.6 g

—PASTA WITH TOMATO PESTO—

3 tomatoes
4 garlic cloves, chopped
Salt and freshly ground black pepper
2 oz. fresh basil leaves
3 oz. blanched almonds
5 tablespoons olive and sunflower oil, mixed
2 recipes Basic Egg Pasta (see page 32)
Extra chopped fresh tomatoes, to garnish

Place all the ingredients except pasta and garnish in a food processor and puree until smooth. Chill in the refrigerator.

Roll out pasta as thinly as possible. Dust with flour and roll up into a sausage shape. Using a sharp knife, cut pasta into ¼-inch slices. Unravel and place on a floured cloth towel until ready to cook.

Bring a large pan of boiling salted water to a boil. Add the pasta and cook 2 to 3 minutes, drain well and toss the pasta with the tomato pesto. Serve immediately with extra chopped tomatoes as a garnish.

Makes 8 servings.

Total Cals: 2990   Total fat: 127 g
Cals per portion: 374   Fat per portion: 15 g

——ONION & ANCHOVY PIZZA——

1 tablespoon active dried yeast
Pinch of sugar
3 cups bread flour
1 tablespoon olive oil
½ teaspoon salt
FOR THE TOPPING :
1 tablespoon olive oil and sunflower oil, mixed
2 lbs. red onions, thinly sliced
2 tablespoons freshly squeezed lemon juice
2 tablespoons chopped fresh oregano and rosemary
8 anchovy fillets in oil, drained, rinsed and sliced
  lengthwise if desired, or 6 anchovies in salt, boned
  and rinsed
10 ripe olives, stoned
Rosemary sprigs, to garnish

In a bowl, dissove yeast and sugar in 1 cup warm water. Let stand 5 minutes. Sift flour into a bowl and make a well in center. Pour in yeast mixture, oil and salt; mix until dough comes together. On a floured surface, knead 10 minutes until smooth. Place in a clean oiled bowl, cover with a damp cloth towel and let rise until doubled in size. To make topping, heat oil in a pan and stir in onions and lemon juice. Cover and cook over low heat until onions are soft. Add chopped herbs.

Preheat oven to 475F (245C). Punch down dough and stretch out to a 12-inch circle on a floured baking sheet. Spread onions evenly over the dough and scatter anchovy fillets and olives over onions. Bake 10 to 15 minutes until crisp and golden, sprinkling the rosemary sprigs over the top for the last 3 minutes. Serve with salad.

Makes 6 servings.

Total Cals: 1886   Total fat: 41.6 g
Cals per portion: 314   Fat per portion: 6.9 g

PIZZA MARGHERITA

1 tablespoon active dried yeast
Pinch of sugar
3 cups bread flour, plus extra for dusting
3 tablespoons olive oil plus extra for drizzling
½ teaspoon salt
8 tablespoons passata (strained crushed tomatoes)
4 oz. part-skim mozzarella cheese, thinly sliced
Pinch of dried oregano
Fresh basil leaves, shredded
Salt and freshly ground black pepper

In a bowl, dissolve yeast and sugar in 1 cup warm water. Let stand 5 minutes. Sift flour into a bowl and make a well in center. Pour in yeast mixture, oil and salt; mix until dough comes together. On a floured surface, knead 10 minutes until smooth. Place in a clean oiled bowl, cover with a damp cloth towel and let rise until doubled in size.

Preheat oven to 475F (245C). Punch down dough and roll out, or stretch with your fingers, to a 12-inch circle on a large floured baking sheet. Spread passata over the dough, avoiding the edges. Scatter cheese, herbs, salt and pepper over the surface. Drizzle with oil. Bake 10 to 15 minutes until golden and crisp. Serve with salad.

Makes 4 servings.

Total Cals: 1719   Total fat: 49.7 g
Cals per portion: 286   Fat per portion: 7.9 g

SAUSAGE RAGU WITH POLENTA

1 lb. fresh Italian sausages
1 tablespoon olive oil
1 medium onion, chopped
2 cups passata (strained tomatoes)
⅔ cup dry red wine
6 sun-dried tomatoes, soaked in hot water then
   sliced
Salt and freshly ground pepper
11 oz. quick-cook polenta
Freshly grated Parmesan cheese (optional), to serve

Squeeze sausage out of skins into a bowl and
break up sausage. Heat oil in a medium
saucepan and add onion. Cook 5 minutes
until soft and golden.

Stir in sausage and cook until browned,
breaking up the lumps with a wooden spoon.
Pour in passata and wine and bring to a boil.
Add sun-dried tomatoes and simmer 30
minutes or until well reduced, stirring occasionally. Season with salt and pepper.
Meanwhile, bring 6¾ cups water to a boil in
a pan with 2 teaspoons salt, then sprinkle in
the polenta, stirring or whisking to prevent
lumps forming. Simmer 5 to 10 minutes
according to the package instructions, until
polenta has thickened like soft mashed
potato, stirring constantly.

Spoon the polenta into 6 large soup plates
and make a dip in the center of each. Top
with the sausage ragu and serve at once,
with grated Parmesan cheese if desired.

Makes 6 servings.

Total Cals: 2326   Total fat: 79 g
Cals per portion: 388   Fat per portion: 13 g

Note: If you can't buy fresh Italian sausages,
use good quality sausages mixed with a little
crushed garlic, black pepper and fennel.

SEAFOOD & SAFFRON RISOTTO

2 pinches of saffron threads
6¼ cups fish stock
1¼ cups dry white wine
12 oz. raw shell-on shrimp
6 baby squid, cleaned and cut into rings
6 fresh scallops
8 oz. fresh venus (baby) clams, rinsed
1 lb. fresh mussels, cleaned
1 medium onion, peeled and chopped
12 oz. arborio rice
3 tablespoons chopped fresh parsley, to garnish

Place the saffron in a small bowl and cover with a little boiling water. Let infuse while you cook the fish.

Bring stock and wine to a simmer, add shrimp; cook 2 minutes. Add squid and scallops and cook 2 minutes. Remove with a slotted spoon and set aside. Add clams and mussels to stock, bring to a boil, and cover. Cook 3 to 5 minutes until opened. Remove and set aside. Place 3 tablespoons stock in a large pan and add onion. Cook gently 5 minutes until softened and the stock has evaporated. Stir in rice and cook 2 minutes until rice looks milky. Add saffron water and a ladleful of stock and simmer until absorbed, stirring.

Continue adding the stock, ladle by ladle, until all but 2 ladlefuls is added, and the rice is tender but still has some bite to it. (This should take about 20 minutes.) Season well. Stir in the remaining stock and seafood and cook gently with the lid on 5 minutes or until piping hot. Transfer to a warmed bowl and sprinkle with parsley. Serve at once.

Makes 6 servings.

Total Cals: 2406   Total fat: 16 g
Cals per portion: 400   Fat per portion: 2.7 g

SICILIAN SARDINES

18 fresh sardines
2 oz. pine nuts, toasted
2 oz. raisins
3 tablespoons chopped fresh parsley
Finely grated peel and juice of 1 orange
Salt and freshly ground black pepper
Bay leaves
¼ cup olive oil

Scale sardines and cut off heads. Slit open the stomachs and remove the viscera under cold running water. Slide your thumb along the backbone to release flesh along its length. Hold backbone at head end and lift it out.

Preheat oven to 350F (175C). Mix together pine nuts, raisins, parsley, orange peel, salt and pepper. Place a spoonful on the flesh-side of each fish. Roll up from the head end and secure with a wooden pick, if necessary.

Place the fish in an oiled ovenproof dish so that they are tightly packed together with the tails sticking up. Tuck a few bay leaves between them. Pour the orange juice and olive oil over them, season well and bake in the oven 10 minutes. Remove wooden picks and serve sardines hot or cold with a tomato and onion salad.

Makes 6 servings.

Total Cals: 1605   Total fat: 139 g
Cals per portion: 267   Fat per portion: 23 g

——SQUID WITH EGGPLANT——

2 cloves garlic, finely chopped
2 tablespoons olive oil
Juice of 1 lemon
1 teaspoon sweet chile sauce
2 small red chiles, seeded and chopped
1½ lbs. baby squid, cleaned, tubes and
   tentacles separated
Vegetable oil for brushing
2 medium eggplants, very thinly sliced
4 oz. arugula
Lemon wedges, to serve

In a bowl, mix together garlic, olive oil, lemon juice, chile sauce and chiles.

Stir squid into marinade, cover and refrigerate 2 hours. Heat a griddle until smoking and brush with oil. Grill eggplant slices in batches 2 minutes on each side. Transfer to a warm oven to keep warm. Remove squid from marinade and reserve the marinade.

Heat griddle until searing hot and fry squid about 20 seconds on each side, then transfer to a plate. Pour marinade into a pan and bring to a boil. Arrange eggplant slices on 4 warm plates. Pile the squid on top and spoon over a little marinade. Surround each portion with a ring of arugula leaves. Serve at once, with lemon wedges.

Makes 4 servings.

Total Cals: 970   Total fat: 47 g
Cals per portion: 242   Fat per portion: 11.9 g

SEA BASS ROASTED WITH FENNEL

1 (2½-lb.) sea bass without head, ready to cook
4 rosemary sprigs and 4 oregano sprigs
3 large fennel bulbs
Salt and freshly ground black pepper
3 tablespoons olive oil
Juice of 1 lemon
4 tablespoons chopped fresh oregano and parsley
⅔ cup dry white wine
8 large green olives, pitted

Preheat oven to 425F (220C). Wash fish inside and out and pat dry on paper towels. Lay it in an oval ovenproof dish. Fill cavity with sprigs of rosemary.

Cut fennel bulbs in half lengthways, cut out core and slice the bulbs thickly. Blanch in boiling salted water 5 minutes. Drain. Whisk oil, lemon juice, chopped herbs, salt and pepper together in a medium bowl. Stir in the fennel, turning until coated. Spoon the fennel over and around the fish, and pour over any remaining marinade. Spoon the wine over top and scatter with olives.

Bake 15 minutes, then spoon the cooking juices over the fish and gently stir the fennel around. Bake 15 minutes. Turn off the oven and leave fish 5 minutes before serving. Garnish with oregano sprigs and serve with mixed rice.

Makes 4 servings.

Total Cals: 1364   Total fat: 58.9 g
Cals per portion: 341   Fat per portion: 14.7 g

——— SKEWERED TUNA ROLLS ———

1½ lbs. fresh tuna, sliced ¼-inch thick
1 tablespoon chopped fresh sage
1 tablespoon chopped fresh rosemary
2 dried bay leaves, crumbled
1 teaspoon dried chile flakes
Salt and freshly ground black pepper
Fresh bay leaves
2 lemons, each cut into 6 wedges
1 tablespoon olive oil
1 tablespoon lemon juice

Soak 4 bamboo skewers in cold water 30 minutes. Meanwhile, preheat broiler or grill. Place tuna slices between sheets of plastic wrap and beat gently with a rolling pin until thin.

Mix sage, rosemary, dried bay leaves and the spices together. Sprinkle mixture over tuna slices and season with salt and pepper. Roll up each slice of tuna neatly. Thread onto bamboo skewers, alternately with the fresh bay leaves and lemon wedges.

Brush with olive oil and lemon juice. Broil or grill 2 to 3 minutes on each side until just cooked. Serve with a green salad.

Makes 4 servings.

Total Cals: 952   Total fat: 32 g
Cals per portion: 283   Fat per portion: 8 g

Variation: Use swordfish instead of tuna. Ask the fishmonger to slice it thinly or buy it in a piece, then chill and slice it yourself.

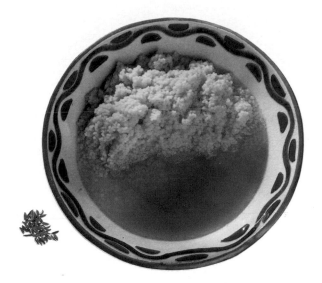

SEAFOOD COUSCOUS

4 lbs. mixed whole, cleaned fish
1 lb. fresh mussels, cleaned
5 tablespoons olive oil
4 medium leeks, washed and sliced
2 medium fennel bulbs, sliced
4 cloves garlic, crushed
1¼ lbs. plum tomatoes, roughly chopped
1 pinch of saffron threads
2 tablespoons sun-dried tomato paste or concentrate
1 teaspoon fennel seeds
½ cup white wine
3 cups fish stock
4 large raw shell-on shrimp
About 18 oz. couscous
Salt and freshly ground pepper

Chop fish, including the bones, into large chunks and place them in a large bowl in the refrigerator. Place mussels in a bowl of cold water. In a large pot, heat oil, add leeks and fennel and cook gently about 5 minutes until softened, then add garlic, tomatoes, saffron, tomato paste, fennel seeds, wine and fish stock. Cover and boil 20 minutes to emulsify the oil. Add the fish and shrimp, bring to a boil again, then partly cover and simmer 20 minutes. Drain the mussels and add them to the soup. Cover and simmer 5 minutes.

Strain soup through a fine sieve or colander lined with cheesecloth into another pan. Discard solids. Season the soup. Cook the couscous according to package instructions. Reheat soup. Place couscous in a warm bowl. Pour over half the soup, cover and rest 30 minutes. Fork up grains and serve in bowls with rest of soup served separately.

Makes 6 servings.

Total Cals: 2039   Total fat: 67 g
Cals per portion: 340   Fat per portion: 11 g

——RED MULLET PACKAGES——

4 (8-oz.) red mullet, ready to cook
2 tablespoons olive oil
4 fresh bay leaves
4 sage leaves
Salt and pepper
4 thin slices prosciutto
Sage sprigs, to garnish

Preheat oven to 375F (190C). Cut 4 rectangles of baking parchment big enough to
wrap each red mullet generously. Brush the
rectangles with the oil. Place a bay leaf in
the cavity of each fish.

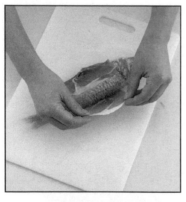

Lay a sage leaf on the side of each fish and
season with salt and pepper. Wrap each fish
in a slice of prosciutto.

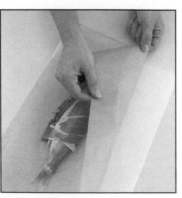

Lay the fish on one half of the paper, fold
over the other half loosely and twist the
edges together to seal. Repeat with all the
other fish. Lay them on a baking sheet and
bake 25 minutes. Serve at once, opening the
packages at the table. Garnish with sage and
serve with broccoli and parsley couscous.

Makes 4 servings.

Total Cals: 928   Total fat: 39 g
Cals per portion: 232   Fat per portion: 9.9 g

─────────TROTA IN BLU─────────

4 very fresh trout, gutted through gills, if possible, taking care not to remove the slime that covers the fish and will make it turn a bluish color when cooked in the vinegar
3 tablespoons wine vinegar
Lemon wedges and parsley sprigs, to garnish
FOR THE COURT BOUILLON:
1 onion, 1 carrot and 1 stalk celery, sliced
2 sprigs each parsley and thyme
1 bay leaf
⅓ cup white wine vinegar
Salt and 4 peppercorns, crushed

Place trout in a dish and sprinkle with the 3 tablespoons vinegar. Cover and chill.

Meanwhile, to make the court bouillon, put onion, carrot, celery, herbs and vinegar in a large saucepan with a little salt, peppercorns and 6¼ cups water. Bring to a boil, reduce heat, cover the pan and simmer 30 minutes. Strain and return to the pan. Heat to barely simmering.

Uncover trout, drop them into the liquid, two at a time, if pan is not large enough to take all of them, and cook 7 to 8 minutes. They will turn a grey-blue and curl slightly. Remove as soon as they are done. Arrange on a platter and garnish with lemon wedges and parsley sprigs. Serve with new potatoes and green beans.

Makes 4 servings.

Total Cals: 784   Total fat: 26.6 g
Cals per portion: 196   Fat per portion: 6.6 g

——ROASTED GRAY MULLET——

1 (3¼ to 3½-lb) gray mullet, cleaned
Salt and freshly ground pepper
1 bay leaf
1 sprig rosemary
6 tablespoons olive oil
Juice of 2 small lemons
1 teaspoon dried oregano
1 tablespoon chopped fresh parsley
2 cloves garlic, finely chopped
Bay leaves and lemon wedges, to serve

Preheat grill or broiler. Season cavity of fish with salt and pepper. Place one bay leaf and rosemary inside the fish.

Grill or broil the mullet over medium heat for about 8 minutes on each side.

Whisk together oil, lemon juice, oregano, parsley and garlic until thick. Lay the fish on a serving platter and garnish with bay leaves and lemon wedges. Pour the sauce over the fish and serve at once, with new potatoes and leeks.

Makes 6 servings.

Total Cals: 1734   Total fat: 104 g
Cals per portion: 289   Fat per portion: 17 g

—MONKFISH IN CITRUS SAUCE—

1¾ lbs. trimmed monkfish, cut into chunks
2 tablespoons flour seasoned with salt and pepper
2 tablespoons olive oil
Finely grated peel and juice of 1 lemon and 1 orange
⅓ cup dry white wine
2 tablespoons chopped fresh parsley
Salt and freshly ground black pepper

Toss monkfish in the seasoned flour and shake off the excess.

Heat oil in a nonstick frying pan, add fish and fry until golden all over. Add the citrus peels and juices and wine, then cook over high heat to evaporate the alcohol. Reduce heat and simmer 3 minutes.

Add chopped parsley and salt and pepper to taste. Lift the fish out and place on a serving dish. Reduce the sauce a little more and pour it over the fish. Serve at once, with new potatoes and sugar snap peas.

Makes 4 servings.

Total Cals: 973   Total fat: 36.5 g
Cals per portion: 243   Fat per portion: 9 g

——MUSSELS ALLA MARINARA——

2¼ lbs. live mussels
1 tablespoon olive oil
4 cloves garlic, chopped
4 tablespoons chopped fresh parsley
½ teaspoon chile flakes
½ cup dry white wine
1¼ cups passata (strained crushed tomatoes)
Salt and freshly ground pepper
Crusty bread, to serve

Scrub and de-beard mussels. Wash in several changes of water and discard any that are not firmly closed.

Put mussels into a large saucepan and place over high heat. Cover and shake pan over the heat until they all open. Transfer from the pan to a bowl. Strain the cooking juices into a cup.

Heat oil, add garlic and cook until golden. Add half the parsley, the chile flakes, wine, passata and mussel liquor. Bring to a boil, season well and add mussels. Heat through 4 minutes, then scatter the remaining chopped parsley over the top. Serve at once, with crusty bread.

Makes 4 servings.

Total Cals: 803   Total fat: 26 g
Cals per portion: 201   Fat per portion: 6.5 g

—MIXED VEGETABLE FRITATTA—

8 oz. fresh asparagus
6 oz. small new potatoes
8 oz. frozen broad beans, thawed
4 eggs
2 egg whites
Salt and freshly ground black pepper
3 tablespoons chopped mixed herbs
3 tablespoons butter
1 oz. freshly grated Parmesan cheese

Trim asparagus. Steam 12 minutes until tender, then plunge into cold water to set the color and cool completely.

Meanwhile, cook potatoes in boiling salted water 15 to 20 minutes until tender. Cool and thickly slice. Slip beans out of their skins. Drain and dry asparagus and cut into short lengths. Mix with beans. Beat eggs and egg whites together with a pinch of salt, and plenty of pepper. Stir in asparagus, beans and herbs. Melt the butter in a 10-inch heavy nonstick frying pan. When foaming, pour in egg mixture. Reduce heat as low as possible and cook about 15 minutes, until set and top is a little runny. Preheat broiler.

Scatter cooked sliced potato over the egg mixture and sprinkle with Parmesan cheese. Place under hot broiler to lightly brown the cheese and just set the top. It should not brown too much or it will dry out. Serve immediately with salad.

Makes 4 servings.

Total Cals: 1128
Cals per portion: 282

Total fat: 75.6 g
Fat per portion: 18.9g

VEGETABLES "A SCAPECE"

12 oz. medium zucchini
12 oz. medium carrots
4 tablespoons olive oil
Salt and freshly ground black pepper
2 tablespoons chopped fresh mint
2 tablespoons white wine vinegar
Extra mint sprigs, to garnish

Trim and diagonally slice the zucchini and carrots, about ⅛-inch thick.

Heat oil in a heavy nonstick frying pan and fry vegetables in batches until golden brown. Remove to a bowl with a slotted spoon as they are ready, leaving any oil in the bottom of the pan. Season vegetables to taste with salt and pepper.

Add mint and vinegar to the pan, bring to a boil and immediately pour the mixture over the vegetables. Toss carefully to mix, then let stand at room temperature at least 30 minutes to allow the flavors to develop. Garnish with extra mint and serve.

Makes 6 servings.

Total Cals: 564   Total fat: 47 g
Cals per portion: 94   Fat per portion: 7.8 g

GLAZED BABY ONIONS

1¼ lbs. pickling onions
4 tablespoons unsalted butter
1 tablespoon sugar
Salt and freshly ground black pepper
⅓ cup chicken or vegetable stock

Peel onions by plunging them into boiling water 1 minute, then drain well and refresh under cold running water and peel off the skins.

Melt the butter in a heavy nonstick pan and add onions in a single layer. Sprinkle the sugar over them and add salt and pepper to taste. Cover and cook over very low heat 20 to 30 minutes until the onions are tender and caramelized, shaking pan often.

dd the stock, bring to a boil and simmer without the lid 5 minutes or until the sauce is syrupy. Serve immediately.

Makes 4 servings.

Total Cals: 582   Total fat: 46.5 g.
Cals per portion: 145   Fat per portion: 11.6 g

─── GARLIC POTATOES ───

1 lb. medium-size waxy potatoes
4 tablespoons olive oil
4 cloves garlic, unpeeled
Few sprigs of thyme or rosemary
Sea salt, to sprinkle
Extra herbs, to garnish

Cut potatoes lengthways into quarters and place in a bowl of cold water. Rinse under cold running water and pat completely dry with paper towels.

Heat oil in a Dutch oven and when smoking hot, add the potatoes and garlic. Reduce heat and brown the potatoes on all sides. Stir in herbs, cover and cook in their own steam 15 minutes.

Remove lid and increase heat to evaporate any water and crisp the potatoes. Turn into a warm serving dish, if desired, and sprinkle with plenty of salt and more herbs.

Makes 4 servings.

Total Cals: 711
Cals per portion: 178

Total fat: 45 g
Fat per portion: 11.3 g

—BRAISED ARTICHOKES & PEAS—

2 tablespoons olive oil
6 green onions, chopped
1 clove garlic, crushed
12 fresh baby artichokes
lemon juice
2 lbs. fresh green peas, shelled, or 10 oz.
  frozen petits pois, thawed
2 tablespoons chopped fresh parsley
Salt and freshly ground black pepper

Heat oil in a Dutch oven, add the onions and garlic and cook over low heat about 5 minutes until beginning to soften. Set aside.

Trim artichoke stalks to about ½ inch. Break off tough outside leaves, starting at the base, until you expose a central core of pale leaves. Slice off tough green or purple tips. With a small sharp knife, pare dark green skin from base and down stem. Cut artichokes in half and brush the cut parts with lemon juice to prevent browning.

Add artichokes and ½ cup water to the onions. Cover and simmer 10 minutes or until almost tender. Gently stir in the peas and a little extra water, if necessary. Cover and cook 10 minutes, if using fresh peas, 5 minutes if frozen ones. Stir in parsley, season to taste with salt and pepper and serve at once.

Makes 6 servings.

Total Cals: 540   Total fat: 26 g
Cals per portion: 90   Fat per portion: 4.3 g

TOMATOES WITH GARLIC CRUST

6 slices stale bread
1 (2-oz.) can anchovies in oil, drained
6 cloves garlic, finely chopped
3 tablespoons chopped fresh parsley
Salt and freshly ground pepper
1½ lbs. small plum tomatoes
3 tablespoons olive oil
Extra chopped fresh parsley, to garnish

Preheat oven to 425F (220C). Tear up bread and place in a food processor with anchovies. Blend bread to crumbs, then dry-fry in a frying pan until crumbs are golden. Stir in garlic, parsley, salt and pepper.

Halve tomatoes and place cut side up, close together in a single layer in a shallow roasting tin or dish. Sprinkle the breadcrumb mixture evenly over tomatoes and drizzle with olive oil.

Bake about 20 minutes until crust is golden and tomatoes are soft. The tomatoes will slightly disintegrate under the crust. Garnish with more chopped parsley and serve at once.

Makes 6 servings.

Total Cals: 951   Total fat: 38 g
Cals per portion: 158   Fat per portion: 6.3 g

──RICE-FILLED TOMATOES──

4 beefsteak tomatoes
Salt and freshly ground black pepper
About 1 cup cooked rice
1 tablespoon pine nuts
1 tablespoon raisins, soaked in hot water
1 stalk celery, finely chopped
2 tablespoons chopped fresh basil
2 teaspoons balsamic vinegar
2 tablespoons olive oil

Preheat oven to 325F (165C). Slice a lid off tomatoes; reserve. Scoop out flesh and sprinkle insides of tomatoes with salt. Invert and drain on paper towels 15 minutes.

Sieve tomato pulp and mix into the cooked rice with pine nuts, raisins, celery and half the basil. Season well and use this to fill the tomatoes. Replace lids and place tomatoes in an oiled shallow ovenproof dish. Bake 45 minutes.

Whisk the vinegar with the oil. Remove the tomatoes from the oven, take off the lids and drizzle each one with the oil and vinegar. Replace the lids and leave to cool. Serve at room temperature, garnished with the rest of the basil.

Makes 4 servings.

Total Cals: 619   Total fat: 35.5 g
Cals per portion: 155   Fat per portion: 8.9 g

TOMATO & EGGPLANT GRATIN

1 medium eggplant
Salt and freshly ground pepper
1 lb. ripe red tomatoes
⅔ cup olive oil
3 tablespoons freshly grated Parmesan cheese

Using a sharp knife, slice the eggplant into ⅛-inch slices. Sprinkle with salt and place in a colander to drain 30 minutes. Rinse well and pat dry with paper towels.

Preheat oven to 400F (250C). Halve tomatoes. Heat oil in a frying pan and fry the eggplant slices in batches until golden brown. Drain on paper towels.

Arrange the tomato halves and eggplant slices in a shallow ovenproof dish. Season with salt and pepper and sprinkle with Parmesan cheese. Bake 10 to 15 minutes until browned. Cool slightly and serve warm.

Makes 6 servings.

Total Cals: 1336   Total fat: 127 g
Cals per portion: 223   Fat per portion: 21 g

FENNEL WITH LEMON & OLIVES

3 large fennel bulbs
Grated peel and juice of 1 lemon
6 tablespoons olive oil
Salt and freshly ground black pepper
12 ripe or green olives
2 tablespoons chopped fresh parsley

Preheat oven to 400F (205C). Trim fennel and cut away any bruised parts. Cut off fibrous tops, halve the bulbs lengthways and cut out the core.

Place the bulbs cut-side up in a baking dish. Finely grate the peel from the lemon, then squeeze the juice. Mix the lemon peel with the juice and olive oil, salt and pepper.

Pour lemon mixture over the fennel, scatter the olives over the top and bake 15 minutes. Turn fennel over and bake 15 minutes. Turn it once more and bake 15 minutes until very soft. Sprinkle with the parsley and serve.

Makes 4 servings.

Total Cals: 712   Total fat: 71.3 g
Cals per portion: 178   Fat per portion: 17.8 g

TUSCAN BEAN & TOMATO STEW

1 lb. dried white haricot or cannellini beans,
   soaked in cold water for several hours or overnight
12 oz. soft, ripe tomatoes or 1 (14½-oz.) can
   chopped plum tomatoes, drained
4 tablespoons olive oil
3 cloves garlic, chopped
3 fresh sage leaves
Salt and freshly ground black pepper
Sage leaves, to garnish

Drain and rinse beans. Place in a saucepan
and cover with cold water. Bring to a boil
and boil 15 minutes. Drain.

Press the tomatoes through a strainer or
puree in a blender, then press the puree
through a sieve.

Heat oil in a large saucepan and add garlic
and sage. Cook over low heat until garlic is
golden brown. Stir in beans, then tomato
puree. Bring to boil, then reduce heat and
simmer 20 minutes or until beans are no
longer crunchy but still firm. Taste and season with salt and pepper. Garnish with sage
leaves and serve at once.

Makes 8 servings.

Total Cals: 1743   Total fat: 52 g
Cals per portion: 218   Fat per portion: 6.5 g

CAPONATA

4 medium eggplants, cubed
Salt and freshly ground pepper
5 tablespoons olive oil
1 medium onion, chopped
6 very ripe red tomatoes, peeled and chopped
6 stalks celery, chopped
1 tablespoon salted capers, rinsed well
2 oz. green olives
3 tablespoons red wine vinegar
1 tablespoon sugar
Chopped fresh parsley, to garnish

Place eggplant cubes in a colander, sprinkle with salt and let stand 30 minutes. Rinse and pat dry.

Preheat oven to 400F (205C). Toss eggplants with oil in a roasting pan and roast 20 minutes until golden brown, stirring occasionally. Remove with a slotted spoon and set aside. Pour the residual olive oil into a saucepan and add onion. Cook 5 minutes until soft. Add the tomatoes and cook 15 minutes until tomatoes are pulpy.

Add all remaining ingredients, except eggplants and garnish, to sauce and simmer 15 minutes. Season well and stir in the eggplants. Allow to stand at least 30 minutes to allow the flavors to develop before serving. Serve warm or cold, sprinkled with parsley.

Makes 6 servings.

Total Cals: 819   Total fat: 65 g
Cals per portion: 137   Fat per portion: 10.8 g

PEPERONATA

3 tablespoons olive oil
2 medium onions, sliced
3 cloves garlic, chopped
2 medium yellow bell peppers
2 medium red bell peppers
2 lbs. fresh tomatoes or 2 (14½-oz) cans
   chopped tomatoes
Salt and freshly ground black pepper

Heat olive oil in a saucepan, add onions and garlic and cook over very low heat at least 20 minutes until golden and caramelized.

Halve and seed bell peppers and cut into thin strips. Add to onions and cook 5 minutes until softened.

Peel, core, seed and chop tomatoes, then stir into pepper mixture. Simmer, uncovered, 30 to 45 minutes until mixture is soft, thick and reduced. Taste and season with salt and pepper. Serve warm or cold.

Makes 4 servings.

Total Cals: 761   Total fat: 38.4 g
Cals per portion: 190   Fat per portion: 9.6 g

——BASIC TOMATO SAUCE——

2 lbs. fresh tomatoes or 2 (14½-oz) cans chopped
  tomatoes, drained
1 medium onion
2 garlic cloves
4 fresh basil leaves, bruised
3 tablespoons olive oil

Rinse fresh tomatoes, cut into quarters and
place in a large saucepan. Chop onion and
garlic and add to tomatoes. If using canned
tomatoes, add to saucepan with onion and
garlic. Cover, bring to a boil, then simmer
25 minutes.

Uncover saucepan and simmer 15 to 30
minutes to evaporate any extra liquid – the
sauce should be quite thick.

Press the sauce through a sieve, or puree in a
blender, then sieve to remove any seeds and
skin. Stir in the basil and oil. The sauce is
ready to use and may be kept in a covered
container in the refrigerator for up to 1
week. Serve hot or cold.

Makes 4 servings.

Total Cals: 467   Total fat: 35.9 g
Cals per portion: 117   Fat per portion: 9 g

DEVILED STEAKS

1 tablespoon olive oil
4 beef fillet steaks, about 4 oz. each
Salt and freshly ground pepper
2 tablespoons sherry vinegar
6 tablespoons dry red wine
4 tablespoons beef stock
2 cloves garlic, chopped
1 teaspoon crushed fennel seeds
1 tablespoon sun-dried tomato paste
Large pinch chile powder
Chopped fresh parsley and parsley sprigs, to garnish

Heat oil in a nonstick frying pan until smoking, then add the steaks.

Cook 2 minutes, turn over and cook 2 minutes for medium/rare steaks. Cook a little longer if well-done steaks are preferred. Remove from the pan, season and keep warm while making sauce. Pour vinegar, red wine and stock into the pan and boil 30 seconds. Stir in garlic and fennel seeds. Whisk in the sun-dried tomato paste and chile powder, to taste. Simmer until the sauce is syrupy.

Place steaks on warm plates. Pour any juices into the sauce, bring to a boil, taste and season. Pour sauce over the steaks. Garnish with chopped parsley and parsley sprigs and serve with grilled tomatoes and roasted diced potatoes.

Makes 4 servings.

Total Cals: 752   Total fat: 32 g
Cals per portion: 188   Fat per portion: 8 g

STEAK WITH TOMATO & OLIVES

4 (4-oz.) beef minute steaks
2 tablespoons olive oil
2 cloves garlic, chopped
1 medium onion, thinly sliced
1 carrot, finely diced
1 (14½-oz) can chopped tomatoes
1 teaspoon balsamic vinegar
½ teaspoon dried oregano
1 tablespoon chopped fresh basil
Salt and freshly ground black pepper
12 Greek-style ripe olives, pitted
Basil leaves, to garnish

Lightly brush both sides of the steaks with a little of the olive oil. Set aside.

In a nonstick saucepan, heat remaining oil and add garlic. Cook over low heat until golden. Add onion, carrot and 2 tablespoons water. Cover saucepan and simmer 10 minutes until onion is soft, stirring once. Stir in the tomatoes, vinegar, herbs, salt and pepper, then simmer, uncovered, 15 minutes until thick and reduced. Stir in the olives and keep warm.

Heat a ridged griddle until smoking and grill steaks 1 minute per side. Remove to 4 warm plates and season with salt and pepper. Serve with the tomato and olive sauce. Garnish with basil leaves and serve with roasted sliced potatoes and broccoli.

Makes 4 servings.

Total Cals: 944   Total fat: 48 g
Cals per portion: 236   Fat per portion: 12 g

──────BEEF IN BAROLO WINE──────

1 (2¼-lb.) beef round roast
6 cloves garlic, crushed
1 onion, roughly chopped
1 carrot, chopped
1 stalk celery, chopped
2 bay leaves
2 large thyme sprigs
2 to 3 peppercorns, lightly crushed
2 cloves
2 allspice berries, crushed
½ cup Barolo wine, or other full-bodied red wine
2 tablespoons tomato paste
⅔ cup beef stock
Salt and freshly ground black pepper

Place meat in a large plastic bag with the garlic, onion, carrot, celery, bay leaves, thyme, peppercorns, cloves, allspice and wine. Shake the bag, seal and refrigerate several hours or overnight, turning meat occasionally. Next day, preheat oven to 325F (165C). Open bag, remove the meat from marinade and pat dry. Heat oil in a Dutch oven and brown the meat all over. Pour in reserved marinade, tomato paste and stock. Cover tightly and bake 2 to 3 hours until beef is tender.

Lift meat out of pan and keep warm. Skim off any fat, remove bay leaves from the sauce. Puree in a blender or food processor until smooth. Taste and season. The sauce should be quite thick; if it is not, boil to reduce it. Slice the meat thinly and serve with the sauce, accompanied by snow peas and polenta.

Makes 8 servings.

Total Cals: 1424   Total fat: 46.9 g
Cals per portion: 178   Fat per portion: 5.8 g

ITALIAN MEATBALLS

6 tablespoons low-fat milk
1 slice bread, crusts removed
1½ lbs. lean ground beef or lamb
6 green onions, chopped
1 clove garlic, chopped
2 tablespoons freshly grated Parmesan cheese
Freshly grated nutmeg
Salt and freshly ground pepper
2 tablespoons olive oil
⅔ cup dry white wine
1 (14½-oz) can chopped tomatoes

Sprinkle milk over the bread in a shallow dish and let soak a few minutes.

Preheat oven to 350F (175C). Put meat into a large bowl and add soaked bread, green onions, garlic, cheese, nutmeg, salt and pepper to taste. Work together until well mixed and smooth. With wet hands, roll into 30 to 36 even-size balls. Heat the oil in a large nonstick frying pan and brown the meatballs in batches, then transfer them to a shallow ovenproof dish. Pour wine and tomatoes into frying pan and bring to boil, scraping up any sediment from the bottom of the pan.

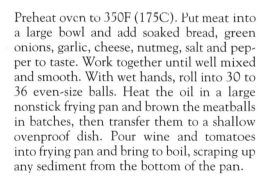

Pour the sauce over the meatballs, cover and bake 1 hour until tender. Serve with buttered noodles.

Makes 8 servings.

Total Cals: 2205   Total fat: 147 g
Cals per portion: 275   Fat per portion: 18.3 g

VEAL SCALOPPINE

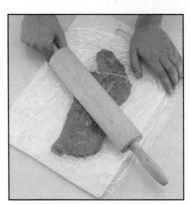

4 (4-oz.) veal or turkey scallops
2 tablespoons all-purpose flour
Salt and freshly ground pepper
3 tablespoons olive oil
3 tablespoons fresh lemon juice
6 tablespoons white wine
2 tablespoons chopped fresh parsley
Lemon wedges, to garnish

Trim veal of any gristle around edge. Place the veal between sheets of plastic wrap and pound out thinly without tearing. Coat in the flour seasoned with salt and pepper.

Heat the oil in a nonstick frying pan. Add veal and fry over high heat about 2 minutes per side, pressing them down with a spatula to keep them flat. Remove from the pan and keep warm.

Add the lemon juice and wine to the frying pan, stirring and scraping to dislodge any sediment. Boil 1 minute, then taste and season. Stir in parsley and pour the lemon sauce over veal. Garnish with lemon wedges and serve at once, with potatoes and stir-fried vegetables.

Makes 4 servings.

Total Cals: 960
Cals per portion: 240

Total fat: 45.8 g
Fat per portion: 11.4 g

SALTIMBOCCA

8 (2-oz.) veal or turkey scallops
8 thin slices Parma ham
Salt and freshly ground pepper
8 fresh sage leaves
1 tablespoon olive oil
2 tablespoons butter
⅓ cup dry Marsala or sherry
Fresh sage leaves, to garnish

Trim veal of any gristle around edge. Place between sheets of plastic film and pound out thinly without tearing. Trim Parma ham of any fat and cut to same size as veal.

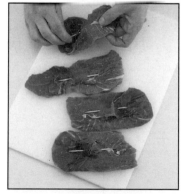

Season veal with a little salt. Place a sage leaf on top of each piece and cover with a slice of ham. Secure each one through the middle with a wooden pick, as if taking a large stitch. These are not rolled up.

Heat the oil and butter in a nonstick frying pan and fry the veal in batches, on both sides for about 2 minutes until golden and tender. Remove and keep warm. Add the Marsala to the pan, stir and bring to a boil, then boil 1 minute. Spoon the sauce over veal, garnish with sage and serve with green beans and noodles.

Makes 4 servings.

Total Cals: 944
Cals per portion: 236

Total fat: 54 g
Fat per portion: 13.6 g

——SKEWERED MEAT ROLLS——

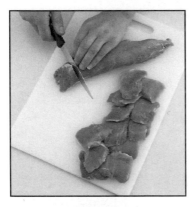

1 (1¾-lb.) lamb, beef or pork tenderloin
8 oz. part-skim low-fat mozzarella cheese
Salt and freshly ground pepper
Fresh basil or sage leaves
2 ears corn
1 eggplant, cut into large cubes
3 medium zucchini, cut into 1-inch lengths
Olive oil for basting

Soak 6 or 12 bamboo skewers in cold water. Cut the meat into thin slices, then place between sheets of plastic wrap and pound out thinly without tearing. Slice cheese thinly.

Season meat with salt and pepper and lay a piece of cheese on top of each piece with a sage or basil leaf. Roll up like a sausage. Place in a dish, cover and chill in the refrigerator.

Meanwhile, cook the corn in boiling salted water 10 minutes, drain and refresh in cold water. Preheat broiler. Slice corn into 1-inch-thick rounds. Thread meat rolls and vegetables onto the skewers. Brush lightly with olive oil, place under the hot broiler and broil 3 to 4 minutes per side. Serve with rice and salad leaves.

Makes 6 servings.

Total Cals: 2232   Total fat: 122.8 g
Cals per portion: 372   Fat per portion: 20.5 g

ROAST LEG OF LAMB WITH WINE

1 (2¼-lb.) lean leg of lamb
2 tablespoons olive oil
1 (2-oz) can salted anchovies, boned and rinsed
2 cloves garlic, chopped
1 tablespoon chopped fresh rosemary
8 juniper berries
2 tablespoons balsamic vinegar
Salt and freshly ground pepper
⅔ cup dry white wine

Trim lamb of any excess fat. Heat oil in a large pan in which the lamb will fit snugly. Add the lamb and brown all over. Remove and set aside.

In a mortar, pound the anchovies, garlic, rosemary and 4 of the juniper berries to a paste. Stir in vinegar. Make small incisions all over the lamb with a small sharp knife. Spread paste all over lamb, working it into the slits. Season. Replace lamb in pan, and pour in wine. Crush remaining juniper berries and add to the pan. Cover and simmer 1½ to 2 hours, until very tender, turning lamb every 20 minutes.

Carefully remove lamb from pan and keep warm. Skim fat from sauce. Add a little water, if necessary, and bring to a boil, scraping the bottom of the pan to mix in the sediment. Serve the sauce with the lamb, accompanied by potatoes, carrots and snow peas.

Makes 8 servings.

Total Cals: 2085
Cals per portion: 260

Total fat: 120 g
Fat per portion: 15 g

——FLORENTINE ROAST PORK——

1 (2¼-lb.) pork loin, boned
2 tablespoons chopped fresh rosemary leaves
2 cloves garlic, chopped
Salt and freshly ground black pepper
3 tablespoons olive oil
⅔ cup dry white wine

Preheat oven to 325F (165C). Using a flat skewer, make deep incisions all over the meat. Mix rosemary and garlic together with plenty of salt and pepper. Push the rosemary mixture into the incisions. Rub any remaining mixture into flap where the bones have been removed.

Season with salt and pepper and tie up neatly with string. Rub meat all over with olive oil and place in a roasting pan. Pour in white wine and roast in oven 1½ hours, basting frequently and turning the roast each time. If you have a spit or rotisserie, roast it on the spit, basting frequently.

Transfer pork to a serving dish and keep warm. Skim fat off pan, and add a little water to the juices. Scrape up sediment and bring to boil, taste and season. Carve the pork into thick slices, garnish with rosemary sprigs and serve with the sauce, carrots and brown lentils.

Makes 6 servings.

Total Cals: 1880   Total fat: 104 g
Cals per portion: 313   Fat per portion: 17.3 g

VENETIAN-STYLE LIVER

3 tablespoons olive oil
4 tablespoons butter
2 large onions, sliced
Salt and freshly ground black pepper
12 slices calf liver
1 teaspooon balsamic vinegar
2 teaspoons white wine vinegar
4 fresh sage leaves, shredded
lemon wedges, to garnish

Heat the oil and butter in a heavy nonstick frying pan and add onions. Cook over low heat about 20 minutes, until onions are very soft and beginning to brown slightly, stirring them occasionally.

Season with salt and pepper, remove with a slotted spoon and keep warm. Increase heat, add liver to pan and fry on each sides 2 to 3 minutes until browned (brown the liver in batches, if necessary).

If browning in batches, return all the liver to the pan. Add the vinegars, sage, salt and pepper to the pan, then add the onions. Toss together to heat through. Garnish with the lemon wedges and serve with zucchini and red lentils.

Makes 6 servings.

Total Cals: 1764   Total fat: 122.5 g
Cals per portion: 294   Fat per portion: 20.4 g

CHICKEN & WILD MUSHROOMS

4 tablespoons olive oil
2 cloves garlic, crushed
4 boneless chicken breasts
⅔ cup dry white vermouth
Salt and pepper
1 lb. mixed wild mushrooms or a mixture of
  cultivated mushrooms, such as brown, shiitake
  and oyster
2 tablespoons chopped fresh oregano
Oregano sprigs, to garnish

Heat half the olive oil in a sauté pan. Add garlic and cook 2 minutes until golden. Add chicken breasts, skin-side down and brown well on all sides.

Pour in the vermouth and season well with salt and pepper. Bring to a boil. Reduce heat, cover and simmer 20 to 30 minutes until tender.

Meanwhile, halve or slice the mushrooms, if large. Heat remaining oil, add mushrooms and sauté 3 to 5 minutes until browned and tender, but still firm. Gently stir mushrooms and any cooking juices into the chicken with the chopped oregano. Garnish with oregano sprigs and serve at once with rice.

Makes 4 servings.

Total Cals: 1442
Cals per portion: 360

Total fat: 79.9 g
Fat per portion: 19.9 g

——LEMON & CHILE CHICKEN——

1 (3¼ to 3½-lb.) free-range chicken,
  cut into 8 pieces
4 ripe juicy lemons
8 cloves garlic
1 small red chile, split, seeds removed, and chopped
1 tablespoon honey
4 tablespoons chopped fresh parsley
Salt and freshly ground black pepper

Place chicken pieces in a shallow ovenproof baking dish. Squeeze juice from the lemons and pour into a small bowl. Reserve the lemon halves.

Remove skin from 2 of the garlic cloves, crush them and add to lemon juice with the chile and honey. Stir well and pour mixture over the chicken, tucking the lemon halves around pieces. Cover and refrigerate at least 2 hours, turning once or twice.

Preheat oven to 400F (205C). Turn the chicken skin-side up and place lemon halves cut-side down around the pieces with the remaining whole garlic. Roast in oven 45 minutes or until golden brown and tender. Stir in the parsley, taste and season. Garnish with the roasted lemon halves and serve with pureed potatoes.

Makes 4 servings.

Total Cals: 1027   Total fat: 38.5 g
Cals per portion: 257   Fat per portion: 9.6 g

—CHICKEN UNDER A BRICK—

1 (4-lb.) roasting chicken, preferably free-range
4 tablespoons olive oil
Salt and freshly ground black pepper
Chopped fresh parsley and lemon wedges, to serve

Using kitchen scissors or poultry shears, cut along either side of chicken's backbone and remove. Place chicken skin-side down, open out and press down hard to flatten. Turn skin-side up.

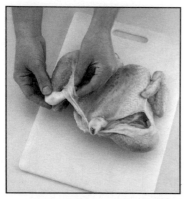

Make a slit through the skin at each side between breast and thigh. Fold the legs in and push the drumstick bone through each slit. The bird should be completely flat. Heat the oil in a large heavy frying pan and place chicken skin-side down in pan. Place a flat lid on top of the chicken and a 10-lb. weight (bricks or stones) on top. Cook 12 minutes over medium heat until golden.

Remove lid and weights, turn chicken over, season well and replace lid and weights. Cook 12 to 15 minutes or until tender and the juices run clear. Let rest in a warm place 15 to 20 minutes before carving. Serve with chopped fresh parsley and lemon wedges, accompanied by new potatoes, carrots and zucchini.

Makes 6 servings.

Total Cals: 1554   Total fat: 87 g
Cals per portion: 259   Fat per portion: 14.5 g

CHICKEN CACCIATORA

4 slices smoked bacon, chopped
4 skinless chicken pieces (1¾ lbs.)
2 cloves garlic, chopped
1 tablespoon balsamic vinagar
1 (14½-oz.) can chopped tomatoes
⅔ cup passata (strained crushed tomatoes)
⅔ cup chicken stock
2 medium onions, roughly chopped
Sprig of rosemary
1 bay leaf
Salt and freshly ground black pepper
8 oz. mushrooms, thickly sliced
Chopped fresh parsley, to garnish

Heat a nonstick frying pan, add bacon and fry until golden. Remove to a deep saucepan with a slotted spoon. In the fat remaining in the pan, fry the chicken pieces until well browned, then add to the bacon. Add garlic to frying pan and cook until golden. Deglaze the pan with the vinegar, scraping any sediment from bottom of pan. Pour in canned tomatoes, passata and stock and bring to a boil. Stir in the onions, rosemary and bay leaf and season with salt and pepper.

Pour mixture over chicken and bring to a boil. Reduce heat, cover and simmer 30 minutes. Stir in mushrooms, cover and simmer 15 minutes. Uncover and simmer 15 minutes to allow the sauce to evaporate and thicken. Garnish with plenty of chopped parsley and serve with ribbon pasta.

Makes 4 servings.

Total Cals: 1320
Cals per portion: 330

Total fat: 44 g
Fat per portion: 11 g

—CHICKEN WITH SALSA VERDE—

4 small skinless chicken breasts
½ cup chopped fresh parsley
1 clove garlic, finely chopped
¼ cup chopped fresh mint
1 tablespoon finely chopped capers
1 tablespoon finely chopped gherkins
Finely grated peel and juice of 1 lemon
⅓ cup olive oil
Salt and freshly ground black pepper

Place chicken breasts in a sauté pan, cover with water and bring to a boil. Simmer over low heat 15 to 20 minutes until cooked. Allow to cool completely in the water.

In a bowl, mix together the parsley, garlic, mint, capers, gherkins, lemon juice and peel. Gradually beat in olive oil and season with salt and pepper. Do not do this in a food processor or the texture will be ruined.

Thickly slice each chicken breast crosswise and arrange on a plate, spoon a little salsa verde over it and serve the rest separately. Serve with salad.

Makes 4 servings.

Total Cals: 1262   Total fat: 94.5 g
Cals per portion: 316   Fat per portion: 23.6 g

—PIGEON WITH CRISP POLENTA—

2 tablespoons chopped fresh sage
1 tablespoon chopped fresh rosemary
Salt and freshly ground black pepper
Scant 1 cup quick-cook polenta
8 pigeon breasts or 4 boneless chicken breast halves
Pinch of ground allspice
1 tablespoon olive oil
1 recipe Basic Tomato Sauce (see page 65)
Rosemary and sage sprigs, to garnish

Bring 2½ cups water to a boil with chopped herbs, salt and pepper. Sprinkle in the polenta, whisking to prevent lumps forming.

Reduce heat and simmer the polenta 5 to 10 minutes, stirring constantly until very thick. Turn out onto a wooden board and shape into a loaf with a spatula. Cool, cover and chill 1 hour. Preheat the broiler. Cut the polenta into 4 thick slices. Brush with some of the olive oil and broil on each side until crisp and golden. Keep warm.

Rub pigeon breasts with the allspice, then brush with a little olive oil. Place skin-side up on broiler pan and broil for 4 minutes. Turn over and broil 2 minutes. Top each polenta slice with 2 pigeon breasts. Garnish with rosemary and sage sprigs and serve with the fresh tomato sauce.

Makes 4 servings.

Total Cals: 1454   Total fat: 65 g
Cals per portion: 364   Fat per portion: 16 g

—RABBIT & RED PEPPER STEW—

2¼ lbs. rabbit pieces
2 tablespoons chopped fresh thyme
2 tablespoons chopped fresh rosemary
2 fresh bay leaves
Juice of 1 lemon
1 tablespoon balsamic vinegar
Salt and freshly ground black pepper
2 tablespoons olive oil
4 red bell peppers, roughly diced
1 (14½-oz.) can strained crushed tomatoes, strained

Place rabbit in a plastic bag with the herbs, lemon juice, vinegar, salt and pepper. Seal and leave to marinate in the refrigerator 2 to 3 hours or overnight.

Heat half the oil in a saucepan and add the bell peppers and cook over low heat about 10 minutes until soft. Stir in tomatoes and season with salt and pepper. Cover and simmer 30 minutes. Remove the rabbit from marinade, reserving marinade, and pat dry.

Heat remaining oil in a frying pan, add the rabbit pieces and fry on all sides until golden. Add the rabbit to pepper sauce. Deglaze the frying pan with the reserved marinade and add to the rabbit. Cover and simmer 20 to 30 minutes until the rabbit is tender. Serve with pasta.

Makes 4 servings.

Total Cals: 1290   Total fat: 52 g
Cals per portion: 322   Fat per portion: 13 g

——WATERMELON GRANITA——

1⅓ cups sugar
2 cinnamon sticks
1¾ lbs. watermelon
Juice of 1 lemon
Mint sprigs, to decorate

Put sugar and cinnamon sticks into a pan with 1¼ cups water. Stir over low heat until sugar has dissolved. Bring to a boil and boil 1 minute. Allow to cool completely, then remove, wash and dry the cinnamon sticks.

Pass the watermelon flesh through a strainer, or mash, then sieve to remove the seeds. Mix watermelon pulp with the cold syrup, adding lemon juice to taste, then chill in refrigerator. Pour into a shallow container to a depth of ¾ inch. Cover and freeze for 1 hour until the liquid has formed an ice rim around the edge and is starting to freeze on the bottom.

Scrape this away with a fork and mash evenly with remaining liquid. Repeat every 30 minutes until mixture forms a smooth consistency of ice crystals. Serve mounded high in chilled glasses (frosted in freezer, if suitable), decorated with mint.

Makes 6 servings.

Total Cals: 1430   Total fat: 2.4 g
Cals per portion: 238   Fat per portion: 0.4 g

COFFEE GRANITA

½ cup finely ground espresso coffee beans
Finely grated peel of 1 lemon
⅔ cup sugar
1 tablespoon fresh lemon juice

Put ground coffee into a pan with 2¼ cups water. Bring to a boil and remove from the heat. Add the lemon peel and leave to infuse 5 minutes. Strain through a coffee filter.

Mix ⅔ cup water with the sugar until dissolved. Stir in infused coffee and lemon juice, let cool, then chill in the refrigerator. Pour into a shallow container to a depth of ¾ inch. Cover and freeze 1 hour until the liquid has formed an ice rim around the edge and is starting to freeze on the bottom.

Scrape away ice rim with a fork and mash evenly with the remaining liquid. Repeat every 30 minutes until the mixture forms a smooth consistency of ice crystals. Serve in chilled glasses (frosted in freezer, if suitable) with a dollop of whipped whipping cream, if desired.

Makes 8 servings.

Total Cals: 591   Total fat: 0 g
Cals per portion: 74   Fat per portion: 0 g

──BISCOTTI & VIN SANTO──

6 oz. whole blanched almonds, toasted
½ cup unsalted butter, softened
1 cup sugar
2 eggs, beaten
Finely grated peel of 1 orange
1½ teaspoons baking powder
½ teaspoon salt
1⅓ cups polenta
About 2¾ cups all-purpose flour
Vin Santo, to serve

Coarsely chop one-third of the almonds and mix these with the whole almonds. Cream butter with the sugar until just mixed. Beat in eggs, orange peel, baking powder and salt.

Stir in polenta, almonds and 1½ cups of the flour. Turn onto a floured work surface and knead to a smooth dough, adding the remaining flour little by little, until the dough is soft not sticky. Divide dough into 4 equal pieces and roll each into a sausage 2 inches wide and ¾ inch thick. Place them on 2 greased baking sheets and bake about 35 minutes until just golden around the edges. Cool 5 minutes.

Cut rolls diagonally into ½-inch-thick slices. Place the slices cut-side down on the baking sheets and bake them 10 minutes until golden brown. Transfer to a wire rack to cool completely. Serve with small glasses of Vin Santo for dipping.

Makes about 50.

Total Cals: 4392
Cals per cookie: 88
Cals per glass Vin Santo: 70

Total fat: 212 6 g
Fat per cookie: 4.2 g

—RICOTTA & COFFEE DESSERT—

12 oz. reduced-fat ricotta cheese, softened
12 oz. reduced-fat cream cheese, softened
1 tablespoon rum
2 tablespoons brandy or Tia Maria
1 teaspoon vanilla extract
2 tablespoons finely ground Italian roast coffee beans
3 tablespoons powdered sugar
⅔ cup whipping cream
2 oz. chocolate, cut into shavings, to decorate

Sieve ricotta and cream cheese together, then beat with a wooden spoon. Do not attempt to do this in a food processor.

Beat in the rum, brandy, vanilla and ground coffee. Taste and add sugar. Carefully spoon mixture into small freezerproof dishes or demitasse cups, piling the mixture high. Place in freezer 30 minutes and transfer to the refrigerator to soften slightly about 10 minutes before serving it. The dessert should be only just frozen or very chilled.

Just before serving, whisk the whipping cream to soft peaks and spoon a dollop on top of each dessert, then sprinkle with chocolate shavings. Place on saucers and serve at once.

Makes 6 servings.

Total Cals: 1868   Total fat: 119 g
Cals per portion: 311   Fat per portion: 19.8 g

STRAWBERRY SORBET

1¼ cups sugar
1 lb. fresh strawberries
1 tablespoon balsamic vinegar

Pour 1 cup water into a saucepan and add the sugar. Cook, stirring, to dissolve sugar, then bring to a boil and boil 1 minute. Cool, then chill in refrigerator. Meanwhile, wash and hull the strawberries. Puree in a blender or food processor until smooth, and pass through a sieve, if desired. Chill the puree.

Stir the syrup into the chilled stawberry purée and add the balsamic vinegar. Freeze in an ice cream maker for the best results.

Alternatively, pour mixture into a shallow freezer tray and freeze until the sorbet is frozen around the edges. Mash well with a fork, beat and refreeze until almost solid. Repeat this twice more. Serve in chilled glass dishes.

Makes 6 servings.

Total Cals: 1118   Total fat: 0 g
Cals per portion: 186   Fat per portion: 0 g

ORANGE SORBET

10 large oranges
1 cup sugar
2 tablespoons orange flower water

Pare the peel from the oranges with a vegetable peeler, avoiding any white pith. Chop roughly. Squeeze the juice from the oranges and strain through a sieve.

Pour ¾ cup water into a saucepan, add the sugar and cook, stirring, to dissolve. Stir in the orange peel, juice, and the orange flower water. Boil rapidly 1 minute. Cool, then chill in refrigerator. Strain the syrup.

Freeze in an ice cream maker for the best results. Alternatively, pour into a shallow freezer tray and freeze until the sorbet is frozen around the edges. Mash well with a fork, beat and refreeze until almost solid. Repeat this twice more. Serve in chilled glass dishes.

Makes 4 servings.

Total Cals: 981   Total fat: 0 g
Cals per portion: 245   Fat per portion: 0 g

—LIGHT VANILLA ICE CREAM—

1 vanilla bean
5 cups low-fat milk
4 tablespoons cornstarch
1½ cups sugar
1 teaspoon vanilla extract

Split the vanilla bean in two and place in a saucepan with 4 cups milk. Heat to boiling point, remove from heat and leave to infuse 20 minutes. Remove vanilla bean, scrape out seeds and whisk the seeds back into the milk.

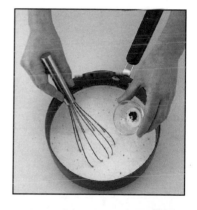

Dissolve the cornstarch in the remaining milk and stir in the sugar. Pour this into the hot milk. Bring to a boil, over medium-low heat, stirring constantly. Cook, stirring, until thickened.

Cover the surface with plastic wrap and allow to cool to room temperature. Stir in the vanilla, chill, then freeze in an ice cream maker for best results. Alternatively, pour into a shallow freezer tray and freeze until ice cream is frozen around the edges. Mash well with a fork, beat and refreeze until almost solid. Repeat this twice more.

Makes 6 servings.

Total Cals: 1802
Cals per portion: 300

Total fat: 18 g
Fat per portion: 3 g

——PEARS POACHED IN WINE——

1 vanilla bean
1¼ cups sweet white wine
1¼ cups Vin Santo
6 firm but ripe dessert pears
2 teaspoons arrowroot
1 teaspoon vanilla extract

Split vanilla bean and place in a saucepan with the wines and bring to a boil. Peel the pears carefully, but leave their stalks on.

Stand the pears in the pan – they should just fit. Spoon a little of the liquid over them to prevent discoloration. Cover tightly and simmer about 25 minutes, turning in the liquid, until tender. Allow pears to cool in the liquid. Remove vanilla bean and scrape out the seeds and reserve them. Lift out the pears and place in a serving dish.

Add vanilla seeds to poaching liquid. Boil until liquid is reduced to 1¼ cups. Moisten arrowroot with a little water and mix into sauce. Boil until thickened. Stir in vanilla. Cool, then pour over pears.

Makes 6 servings.

Total Cals: 996   Total fat: 1.2 g
Cals per portion: 166   Fat per portion: 0 g

Note: Decorate with chopped nuts and mint if desired, but this will add extra calories.

CARAMEL ORANGES

4 large oranges
½ cup sugar
1¼ cups fresh orange juice
1 tablespoon orange liqueur

Remove the peel from the oranges, then remove pith as you would an apple, being careful not to leave any of the white pith behind. Cut the peel into fine julienned strips.

Slice each orange horizontally into rounds and re-form into oranges with the help of a wooden pick. Place in a serving dish. Put the sugar into a heavy pan and add ¼ cup of the orange juice. Heat gently to allow the sugar to melt and dissolve slowly, then boil until it turns a rich golden brown. Remove from heat and add the remaining orange juice, taking care as it will splutter.

Return to heat again, add the peel and stir until caramel has dissolved. Bring to a boil and boil until reduced and syrupy. Cool, then stir in the liqueur. Pour mixture over the oranges and serve.

Makes 4 servings.

Total Cals: 816   Total fat: 0.9 g
Cals per portion: 204   Fat per portion: 0 g

—FEATHER-LIGHT TIRAMISU—

3 tablespoons very strong cold espresso coffee
1 teaspoon vanilla extract
1 tablespoon brandy or rum
⅓ cup vanilla sugar (see page 94)
2 egg whites
8 oz. reduced-fat cream cheese, softened
½ cup reduced-fat crème fraîche or plain yogurt
18 lady fingers
2 oz. dark chocolate, grated

In a bowl, mix together coffee, vanilla and brandy. In another bowl, beat sugar and cream cheese together. Whisk crème fraîche until just holding its shape and fold into the cream cheese mixture.

In a clean bowl, whisk the egg whites until forming soft peaks, then fold into the cheese and cream mixture.

Break half the lady fingers into pieces and place on the bottom of 6 glasses. Drizzle with half the coffee mixture. Spoon on half the cream mixture and sprinkle with half the grated chocolate. Repeat with remaining ingredients, finishing with grated chocolate. Chill until firm and serve within 1 day.

Makes 6 servings.

Total Cals: 1689   Total fat: 73.8 g
Cals per portion: 282   Fat per portion: 12 g

—BAKED RICOTTA CHEESECAKE—

12 oz. reduced-fat ricotta cheese
3 eggs, separated
½ cup sugar
3 tablespoons dark rum
1 teaspoon vanilla extract
finely grated peel of 2 lemons
2 oz. ground almonds
2 oz. golden raisins, soaked in warm water and
  drained
Fresh seasonal fruit, to serve

Preheat oven to 350F (175C). Grease, lightly flour and line bottom of an 8-inch springform pan. Sieve the ricotta into a large bowl and beat in the egg yolks and sugar.

Beat in rum, vanilla and lemon peel. Fold in ground almonds and raisins. Whisk the egg whites until soft peaks form, then gently fold them into the cheese mixture. Gently spoon into prepared pan and level the surface. Bake 30 to 40 minutes until firm and slightly shrunken from the sides of the pan.

Open the oven door, turn off heat and leave cheesecake inside to cool completely, then chill in refrigerator. To serve, remove cheesecake from pan and top with seasonal fruit. Dust with powdered sugar, if desired.

Makes 6 servings.

Total Cals: 1679   Total fat: 89 g
Cals per portion: 280   Fat per portion: 14.8 g

ZABAGLIONE

4 egg yolks
2½ oz. vanilla sugar
½ cup Marsala
Lady fingers, to serve

With an electric whisk, whisk the egg yolks and sugar together in a large heatproof bowl until pale and fluffy. Place bowl over a pan of gently simmering water. Mix in the Marsala.

Start whisking slowly. Gradually whisk faster until the mixture doubles in volume and becomes very thick and glossy. Take care not to overheat or the mixture will scramble.

Spoon the zabaglione into heatproof glasses or ramekins and serve immediately with lady fingers.

Makes 6 servings.

Total Cals: 683   Total fat: 22.5 g
Cals per portion: 114   Fat per portion: 3.7 g

Note: To make vanilla sugar, simply store a vanilla bean in a jar of sugar and leave at least 2 to 3 weeks for it to flavor the sugar.

WALNUT CAKE

12 oz. walnut pieces
1¼ cups sugar
4 eggs, sparated
Finely grated peel of 1 lemon
Powdered sugar, to decorate

Preheat oven to 350F (175C). Grease, flour and line bottom of a 9-inch springform pan. Grind the walnuts in a blender or food processor with 2 tablespoons of the sugar until fine but not greasy.

With an electric beater, whisk the egg yolks and remaining sugar together until pale and creamy. Fold in the lemon peel and walnuts. Whisk egg whites until stiff and carefully fold into the walnut mixture. Gently pour into prepared pan.

Bake 45 to 60 minutes until risen and firm. Cool in the pan. It will shrink away from the edges. Remove from the pan and dredge with powdered sugar. Serve in thin wedges with low-fat vanilla custard, if desired.

Makes 12 servings.

Total Cals: 3653   Total fat: 265.8 g
Cals per portion: 304   Fat per portion: 22 g

INDEX